Raising Mario Twice

Raising Mario Twice

How Love Can Transform a Life After a Tragic Event

Christine Scharmer

iUniverse, Inc.
New York Bloomington

Raising Mario Twice
How Love Can Transform a Life After a Tragic Event

iUniverse books may be ordered through booksellers or by contacting:

iUniverse
1663 Liberty Drive
Bloomington, IN 47403
www.iuniverse.com
1-800-Authors (1-800-288-4677)

ISBN: 978-1-4401-7178-9 (pbk)
ISBN: 978-1-4401-7179-6 (ebk)

Printed in the United States of America

iUniverse rev. date: 10/15/2009

Acknowledgments

I dedicate this book to my husband Mark Scharmer, and my two sons Mario and Miguel. Thank you Mark for being my rock of stability. You stood by me when many men would have fled. Thank you Mario for deciding to live and for working so hard to rehabilitate. Thank you Miguel for your beautiful poetry, it enriches our story.

I'd like to thank the following people for all their help with "Raising Mario Twice"

First I would like to thank my editor and friend Gary Moring who was another answer to my prayers. Gary's editing kept my voice and helped the story flow.

To my parents Bette and Jim Boman who have always supported me through the rough times. To my brother Marc who took the time to proofread the book and lovingly sent the latest information on TBI off the Internet when Mario was first hurt.

To my friends Sandra Dax, LaRae Foushee, Maryann Kachur and Geri Dockter, who were the first to read the manuscript and encourage me to publish the book.

A special thank you to all the healers that have worked with Mario: Virginia MacDonald, Nancy Fitzgerald, Barb Fors, Solon Vargas, Libby Luxemberg, Lucy Heart, Dr. William King, Sharon Wise, Dr. Kostecki Sani, Dr. Smith, Ron Tura, Gayle den Daas, Simone St. Clare, and Sheri Miller.

Thank you Gina and Nicole Russo for being Mario's friends and supporting him that first year when he needed you the most.

To our supporting friends Michelle and Michael Poston, Sam Foushee, Bart and Hazel Bright, Richard Allen, Steve Galleon. Curtis Braxton, Marie Chellino, Tom Krehbiel, Ellen Gillan, Carol Warren, Pat McDonald, Karen Goldman, Simone St. Clare, Tony Bradley, Kathleen Ely, Eric Sligar, and Ken Bartizal

To Mario and Miguel's Aunt Irma and Uncle Jim, Uncle Alfredo, Aunt Maryann and Grandmother Helen Scharmer.

To the Valhalla staff and principal, Marji Calbeck for your loving support the five years I worked after the accident.

I have been richly blessed with loving care providers and am grateful for them all: Stephanie Sanchez, Ana Roman, Ana Sacco, Shayla Wilkensen, Kelly Maitland, Eric Johansen, Debra Jacobson, David Wright, Nick Duncan, Kat Brown, Amanda Reganit, and Walter Zintz.

Thank you Kris Carlson for your beautiful words in the forward of this book and for helping raise Mario the first time around. To her daughters Kenna and Jasmine for their love, prayers, and visits when Mario was hurt.

A big thanks to Richard Carlson who promised to help me with the book and did so in spirit. You will never be forgotten.

Thank you to the hundreds of people who prayed for Mario and have helped with "Raising Mario Twice." I am grateful for you all.

Forward by Kristine Carlson,
Author of *Don't Sweat the Small Stuff for Women,*
Co-Author with Richard Carlson of *Don't Sweat the Small Stuff in Love*
and *An Hour to Live, An Hour to Love.*

There are moments we just remember like they happened yesterday. I was on a bike on back roads in Montana when Richard called. He said: "There's been a terrible accident. Mario is in the hospital fighting for his life. He's in a coma, Kris, and it doesn't look good. They think he was dead on arrival."

The Scharmer family had been our neighbors for twelve years. Sharing a parallel spiritual path, we had become more like family than neighbors. The boys, Mario and Miguel, spent much time with us while growing up. They would sometimes spend the night in our guestroom and hang out with our daughters Jasmine and Kenna when they were little. Even as Mario and Miguel grew into young adult men, we still remained bonded and we knew we had their respect. Just that week before Mario's crash, he had come to our door and asked Richard to help him lift his engine into the shell of his truck. They shared a male bonding moment as they mustered the strength to lift the heavy equipment in teamwork. They laughed and high-fived at their success.

Now, as I turned the pedals of my bike, I was no longer present to the beauty of the Montana Mountains. I felt deep concern for Chris as I felt her pain as a mother, that she very well might lose her son. I also considered what life might be like if he lived.

Chris and Mark had really been put to the test with their boys. Both boys had a wild streak, with more than their share of testosterone, they were challenging on all levels. They tested every boundary and went through incredible periods of disrespect. I often felt disappointed in both of them, that they couldn't see beyond their actions. Given their loving upbringing and exposure to the spiritual world, I just hoped they would survive their egos long enough to find their way back to spirit and the value system of their mother.

There was never a time when Richard and I were not amazed at how Chris and Mark rose to the challenge before them with Mario. These circumstances were the most demanding imaginable and Chris called on all her past work and training, spiritual and otherwise, to utilize the tools in her emotional and spiritual tool belt. The years of spiritual study, meditation and prayer paid off for her in dividends as she intuited a healing process through uncharted territory. How the brain heals is still very much a medical mystery. At the time, the Doctors said, "Mario, will likely be a vegetable. Chris responded with one word: "No!" She knew in her heart that all things are possible through the miracle of love.

In the early months, I'll never forget how she designed her own program to stimulate new neural pattern development in Mario's brain. She created a schedule of volunteers and had all sorts of sensory development stimuli available for us to use on our visits. I would wash my hands really well, enter Mario's hospital room and spend a few moments just talking to him to let him know I was there. Then, I would read the notes available on what the previously scheduled visitor did and I would mix it up by picking up the next series of items in the box. There were feathers, musical instruments, aromatherapy oils, brushes and many things that would engage Mario's five senses as if for the first time. I marveled to see Chris travel this journey as she had many years earlier as a kindergarten teacher. Mario was back in Kindergarten again.

Mario remained unconscious except for his heartbeat monitor. Among the most powerful intuitions she had, Chris realized Mario communicated through his heart rate monitor and his heart beat.

There were many things that struck Richard and I as we witnessed Chris and Mark stand up and refuse to be knocked down. They became two of the most devoted parents on the planet. Many would have given up, being completely overwhelmed from the shock and hardship they were facing.

Chris, Mark and Miguel, bonded together and stayed completely present with hope that was imminent and a belief in God that offered strength and encouragement. They have always refused to believe anything other than Mario having a full recovery.

They were unwilling to compromise Mario's life in any way. They have been a testament, not only to love, but to the bonds of family and the courage it takes to face the suffering of a loved one. Through their example, they have shown how a spiritual practice can be a way of life and how that life style deals with loss and the most demanding of circumstances.

Over the years, I have come to realize that the experience of tragedy and suffering in our lives contains with in it the incredible potential to awaken and ignite our spiritual calling. Our lives may end up having more meaning for change in our world than they would have otherwise if everything had worked out according to our own tidy plan. When we say, "Yes" to spirit, we cannot hide as spirit moves us, as spirit often will. Chris said, "Yes" long ago. Mark said, "Yes" when he married Chris and adopted Mario and Miguel.

As Mario surrendered to his circumstances, he has become a teacher of love. Everywhere he goes he touches people through his incredible exuberance for life. He smiles and kisses and offers unadulterated joy through his essence. He has meaning and purpose and he is loved and he loves. Is it easy to be him? Not one moment of any day is this an easy life for him or any of the Scharmers. They smile and enjoy what life has given them with gratitude. Their courage touches you. The main message here is that love can transform any circumstance and as long as we stay present, love will also be there to heal and transform our lives.

Contents

Introduction

We often make plans to do things and just when we're ready to carry them out, life happens. That's what Christine Scharmer told me once; she's the author of this book. And life happened to her in an unexpected way that changed her plans drastically one night, seven years and a thousand lifetimes ago.

This book is about that night and everything that has happened since then. It's the story of a young man's miraculous recovery from death's door. It is also the chronicle of a mother's love for her son as well as the incredible journey she and her family have taken in "Raising Mario Twice."

At the center of this story is Mario himself. The young man who is no longer the same person he was before the crash and who is now a walking testament to how one person can lovingly impact those around him.

I had the honor and privilege of editing this book for Christine and through that process became acquainted with the immense strength of character that she and so many of her family and friends exhibited throughout this ordeal. As her editor I felt that it was important to keep "her voice", something that can be easily lost if a book is over-edited.

Christine has a great way of expressing herself and her narrative description of events will often reveal her inner thoughts and feelings in her own unique way. It was also important to keep the tone and quality of the chapter written by her son Miguel, whose eye- witness account describes the night that this horrendous event unfolded.

At the beginning of each chapter, Christine has included some passages of poetry that her son Miguel has written since the accident. These pearls of insight add great depth to the story. In some cases you'll hear from Mario too, revealing the fact that there is so much inside of him that yearns to touch the hearts of those around him.

In the end, this book is about the miraculous healing power of love, the love bestowed upon Mario by his mother, his family and his friends. But it also about the ongoing impact that Mario has upon the people he meets and how the love that he shares with them changes their lives forever.

Gary Moring
July 2009

CHAPTER 1

Last Words

The tears I shed leave trails of sad spots,
Which in turn release thoughts of my brightest hours
and darkest days.

Miguel Scharmer

My last words to Mario that night were "Stay home. Please don't go. It is too late to go to San Francisco."

I didn't need another sleepless night worrying about my boys. I thought all this was behind us. Oh no, not again.

August 8, 2002. The past seven years had been a rough time with the two boys and now my husband and I were getting ready for the good times. We had been through smashed cars, trips to police stations and school embarrassments, from cutting class to fighting and stealing. Now both our boys had graduated from high school and were enrolled in massage school! Could it be that all our hard work, counseling, tears and late nights worrying about them were finally over?

Mario in particular was the most difficult. He had gone from a dream child, the teacher's pet, and a mamma's boy, to a "Wild Thing." He was completely out of control. Tough love and counseling had been to no avail. It was nine months in the Boy's Farm that finally straightened him out, but that is another story.

The carrot on the stick was in front of my husband and me and we were finally close enough to take a bite. Both boys, Mario eighteen and Miguel twenty-one, were making plans as well. By fall they wanted to move into their own place, finish massage school, and enroll at Diablo Valley College, our local community college. In two years they would transfer to San Diego State. My husband and I couldn't be happier.

We were both worn out from parenting and were looking forward to an empty house and vacations alone. I was fifty now and wanted to focus on my life. I couldn't wait to begin to renew, refresh and enjoy the remaining years that I had. Funny how life happens while you are making other plans.

Mario was home and had just finished eating. We had been keeping him busy with chores, painting the pool house, yard work, and errands. He was not a happy camper. Since he had not been living at home for the past year we thought it a good idea to compose a list of rules or agreements for him to follow. The agreements were for both boys to sign, so we could live together in peace until they moved out. Mario was not happy about signing the paper. He did so, but reluctantly.

Dinner was finished. It was about 9:00 PM when the phone rang and I was getting ready for bed. Miguel called about a bonfire party in San Francisco at Ocean Beach and needed Mario to come and bring his truck. Apparently a whole crew of kids were going out that night. Mario loved to party and I knew that it would be impossible to keep him from taking his truck and going to Ocean Beach. Mario was a real Casanova and had a harem of female admirers. He loved to be the center of attention and the girls always flocked to him.

But we were concerned about Mario's drinking and driving. Miguel, his older brother, had received a DUI at nineteen and we had hoped all the trouble he had gone through might caution Mario. We were terribly wrong. Mario went out that night. It was the last time I saw my boy whole and complete, that beautiful, beautiful boy.

CHAPTER 2

The Party: As Remembered by Mario's brother, Miguel

Fallen star, broken wish, mended heart and stolen kiss,
Tortured souls and restless nights,
Empty pockets and drunken fights,
My past is not who I am.

Miguel Scharmer

My brother Mario had graduated from high school and the two of us were making plans. We shared similar interests and ran with the same crowds. We were partiers and very social. You could say we were known for being wild and crazy and would rev up the life of any social atmosphere with our presence. Together we were unstoppable. It was summer and our phones were always ringing with offers of things to do, along with invitations to barbecues, parties, and road trips. You name it and we were there doing it.

Mario was a very social person. He knew how to encourage good conversation and the women always gathered around him. I shared a similar personality, but needed to put in a little extra work to catch the girls. My looks alone usually didn't seal the deal. But put the two of us together in the same vicinity and you might want to bring your video camera, 'cause things were bound to get interesting.

Our plan was to move out, share an apartment, and go to Diablo Valley College together. But before this all happened, we wanted to enjoy a kick-ass summer. We had similar work schedules and a little money saved up. That would give us the time to enjoy every minute of the last part of our summer freedom.

The day started out as any other day. I'd wake up to the sound of a buzzing alarm clock. You see, I had a little routine of setting it to go off early and hitting the snooze button to silence it, but not shut it off. This put the alarm on delay for about five minutes and it would go off again later. I would let this happen about three our four times until I could finally make myself get out of bed.

Then came the morning rituals. This usually included walking half-awake to the bathroom to release a full bladder, followed by washing my face and brushing my teeth. These things taken care of, I'd hop onto the couch in the living room, flip the television on, and try to think of what I wanted to eat and if I was going to be too lazy to make it.

The phone rang and I got up to answer it. It was my buddy Brad. "What's up?" Brad asked.

"Shit, I'm just lounging round the house," I said.

"Come through to my house, I'm having a barbecue," Brad said.

"Okay, I'll be over there in a bit," I replied.

Of course, Mario wanted to come too, but our parents had him painting the pool house. My parents had lent him $1500 to buy a truck and he worked off some of the money by doing jobs around the house. I got dressed and left for Brad's.

When I arrived, Brad staggered over to my car and greeted me. He had an empty beer bong in his hand and wet spots all over his tee shirt from some of the beer.

"Hey dude, where's Mario?" Brad asked.

"He had to stay home and paint. He might catch up with us later," I replied.

Brad held up the beer bong and said, "You're next. You have got to catch up."

Back then I was crowned the "Beer Bong King" and I was the fastest drinker of all. So I accepted the challenge to catch up and headed into Brad's back yard.

The back yard was filled with familiar faces. I greeted all of our friends and looked around to see two, thirty packs of beer and a couple bottles of vodka. My buddy Dan was on barbecue duty and was grilling it up. I got into the circle on the lawn where the action was going down and got into my beer bong position. I knelt down, put my hand on the release valve and with the other hand, held the tube for balance. I was ready to take down two and a half beers in about seven to nine seconds. I opened the valve and down it went. The cold, frosty beer shot down my throat and into my belly.

"Go, Go, Go, Go," everyone yelled, cheering me on.

I finished and let the foam drip out. A loud belch released and it helped my stomach settle.

The beer bong kept rotating to the next willing participant throughout the day. By the time we finished all the drinking and eating, it had started to get dark. It had been such a kick-ass party; I thought that it would be great to keep it going.

So I yelled, "Let's go to Ocean Beach and throw a bonfire party."

Everyone was up for it, so I called Mario to see if he wanted to go. He had just finished dinner and was anxious to get out of the house and party. I went to the house, changed clothes, picked up Mario and stocked up on wood and stuff.

"Whoever wants to roll meet back at Brad's house at 11:00 P.M.," I said.

Mario's truck was a 1973 Maroon colored Chevy with a camper shell. The back of the bed was carpeted. It was the "Love Shack" on wheels. We called it the "Shaggin' Wagon," 'cause on many nights some guy was getting lucky back there with some pretty girl. The only bad thing about it was that it had no power steering and the brakes were not very good. It had been upgraded with a new stereo system and new speakers.

Most of the day we had been listening to R&B, Hip-Hop, or Metallica's *Black Album*, when we wanted to get amped. That got our blood pumping. So for tonight's music, it just depended on what mood we were in and who was riding DJ. Riding DJ, for those of you who don't know, is the passenger in the car who is closest to the radio or CD controls. That way the driver can concentrate on the road and not the radio. Also, it was kind of a tradition.

When I arrived back at home the family dogs greeted me as soon as I entered. I played and roughed them up a little and headed to the fridge to see if there was anything good to drink or snack on. This is sort of a habit when I get home. Whether I'm hungry or thirsty doesn't matter too much. I'm not sure why I do it. But nothing stood out. It's usually the same old health and protein stuff, like soymilk, tofu, and all kinds of fat-free and organic items. Mom's sort of a health nut.

No red meats in the house either. The closest thing to red meat was chicken, turkey, or fish. If we had something like Martinelli's apple cider, that was a jackpot.

Mario wanted to know who all was going and was anxious to leave. Mom pleaded with us to not go. She felt it was too late, and besides, it wasn't even the weekend yet. Mario got on the phone and talked to some girls about going to the beach. There were a couple of house parties going on too, so there were lots of options. We might change plans at the last minute if we wanted to.

While Mario was on the phone I went to my room to pick out an outfit to wear for the night. I liked to keep my clothes looking nice and straight so I would usually iron before going out. But tonight no ironing would be needed 'cause I didn't want to wear anything too nice going to the beach. Whatever I decided to wear would probably end up getting dirty. I laid out a couple of options on the bed, and then went to the garage to find the big green ice chest. This we'd fill up with as much ice and beer as possible.

I made a list of all we would need so nothing would be forgotten. We also needed a portable CD player and eight size C batteries. Chips and snacks would be nice as well as some kind of chaser for the hard alcohol. The most important thing to grab was lots of wood. Once you run out of wood and the fire dies out, it's too cold to stick around. It's safer to bring too much rather than not enough. I grabbed Mario to help me load up the truck with all the supplies. After we had finished loading we went inside to fill our stomachs. Eating a good meal before going out to party is essential. I don't like drinking on an empty stomach. We ate and headed over back to Brad's house.

When we got to Brad's house we rallied up all the homies and discussed a liquor run to Safeway. We passed a hat around and everybody donated about ten to fifteen dollars. I got all the money sorted out and headed over to Safeway. We grabbed two, twenty-four packs of beer, a bottle of Southern Comfort, Dr Pepper for a chaser, C- batteries for the boom box, chips and ice. Now we were ready. There would be two vehicles going. Most of us were riding in Mario's "Shaggin' Wagon." The brothers, Dan and Joe, along with Sam, were taking the Toyota Tercel. We still had to pick up John and his girlfriend Marie, who lived down the street.

A weird thing happened that night when we arrived at John's

house. While we were waiting for him to gather his belongings I looked out across the street and noticed an older lady standing in her doorway. The car windows were rolled down and our eyes made contact. She said something, but I didn't hear her very well.

"What?" I asked.

"Are you boys going out drinking tonight?" she asked.

"Ya-so-why?" was the response she got.

"I don't think you should go out tonight. It's not a good night to be going out late," she said.

"Okay-whatever," I replied.

Just then we were all thinking, "What is taking John so long?"

I went inside and told him to hurry his lagging ass up. I opened the door and he was already walking over.

" Hurry up fool, let's go already," I said impatiently.

"Alright, I'm good," he said.

Next we went to Marie's house.

"What's up Marie?" I said just to be polite.

Marie and I were friends, but had never really been too close. I mostly just thought of her as John's girlfriend. We opened the camper shell and they climbed into the back. No seat belts back there, but hey; living on the edge is what we did. The windows were tinted so we didn't worry about police seeing us and pulling us over.

We hopped on the freeway and headed toward San Francisco. It usually took us about thirty minutes to get to the tollbooth. We were bumping some Bay hits and just kicking back. We got to the tollbooth and paid the bridge fare. Ocean Beach here we come! After a few more tracks of songs went by, we arrived at the beach parking lot. You could see bonfires all over. We could tell where and who had the biggest ones, so we were peeping the scene, checking out the fires. First things first!

We carried some wood down to a nice spot and had a couple people assigned to making a fire. The others set up blankets and carried down coolers and things. Brad and I grabbed as much wood as we could and walked down the sandy stairs that led into the endless looking beach of darkness. We found a good spot to set up shop. I wanted to get the fire going ASAP, because it was cold and windy.

My Dad Mark, an outdoors type of guy, had shown me how to make a good campfire when I was younger. So I was confident I could get it going. I grabbed a few skinny logs and started stacking them in the shape of a tee pee. After I had what looked like a solid structure, I grabbed the newspaper we had brought along and started ripping pages in half and crumpling them into little balls. The balls were placed in the middle of the tee pee. Things were looking OK so far. The last thing needed to assist in getting the fire going was kindling. We searched for twigs or any loose branches small in size. This would be placed over the newspaper, and once it started burning, it would get the bigger wood to catch on fire. Usually I don't need lighter fluid to start it up, but when you're at the beach, it's good to have, just in case it gets a little damp. I squirted some lighter fluid, grabbed a lighter and set the wood ablaze. It worked great.

"Yeaaaaah, who's the man?" I said.

Brad grinned and replied, "Whatever, I coulda done that."

I glanced up and saw the crew walking toward us with all our supplies. Blankets were thrown down, along with the coolers, boom box, bags of chips, cups, and beer bong. We were all set for what was supposed to be a great night. Let the party begin.

At Ocean Beach in the summer, there will usually be multiple bonfires going on all over the beach. People tend to walk from bonfire to bonfire, drinking and socializing as they go. We took pride in trying to have the biggest fire on the beach and nine times out of ten we did. Things were going smoothly. Everyone was drinking and having a good time. A game of King's Cup was in order, so I opened up a deck of cards. As the gang spread around the cup in the center, I couldn't help but wonder who would end up picking the last king and having to drink the cup. This game never failed to get things flowing and it was fun, too.

King's Cup is a great drinking game. The rules are simple. Each person draws a card one after another and flips it over. Every card has a meaning to it. Most of them are drinking penalties. Whenever someone draws a king he pours some of his drink into the cup. The last king to be drawn from the deck loses and drinks the cup. While we were playing, John got up and walked off toward the water.

"I got to go take a piss, I'll be back," he said.

He left and we resumed playing our game.

Out of the darkness two guys walked over to our site. They strolled over to where John had been sitting earlier and started introducing themselves, engaging in a conversation with Johns girlfriend, Marie. Nobody paid them much attention. Marie told us that one of those guys tried to grab her ass, but that she handled it. It was not a big deal and we shouldn't say anything to John about it. The two guys made an excuse to leave and started to walk off.

John eventually returned and we told him what happened. He became furious.

He said, "Which way did they go?"

We pointed and said, "They walked that way."

John darted off into the night like a mad man after them. We followed him, just as he caught up to them. Words were exchanged and punches were thrown. A scuffle broke out. It ended with them on the ground and all of us fleeing, to avoid running into any law enforcement. We all ran to where the bonfire was and told everyone that was there to pack our shit up. We had to roll out as soon as possible. We grabbed all our stuff and hopped into Mario's truck and skipped out. Marie was in the back with us and she was full of tears, calling everyone jerks and saying that that was exactly what she did not want to have happened.

"That's why I said not to tell him," she stammered.

Overhearing, John replied, "Aw whatever, I don't give a shit. He deserved to get whopped. He grabbed your ass."

We headed toward the freeway for what seemed like a long ride home. Mario's gas was low, so we stopped at a gas station not long after we left the beach parking lot. All the guys jumped out to stretch their legs and used the bathroom. Mario headed over toward the till to pay for gas, but couldn't find anyone to help. I guessed they were closed and just left the light on. This got all the guys rowdy and irritated. Someone grabbed the price stand and threw it toward the entrance and a couple garbage cans were knocked over. We got back into the truck and left. I'm sure that at this point, having to be the driver and all, really stressed Mario out. He didn't say much -- just stuck the key into the ignition and turned the engine over and off we went.

The next thing I remembered was that we were back in town and dropping off passengers at John's house. The final stop was at Brad's house only a few miles away. We wanted to wind down, so when we got there, we parked the truck and chilled outside at the end of the street. The CD of choice for that moment was Metallica, the *Black Album*.

We all had lots of energy so we started doing push-ups on the concrete sidewalk and challenging each other. Time went by and Brad asked if we were sleeping over.

"I'm down," I said.

Mario was hesitant and then said, "Nah, I don't want to leave my truck here, I want to drive back to the house."

"You good to drive?" Brad asked.

"Yeh, I'm good," he said back.

"I guess I will just follow him in my car then," I said to Brad.

We said our goodbyes and I hopped into my Honda CRX and Mario got into his truck. We pulled out of Brad's street one after another.

It was a familiar drive for the both of us, one that we had made hundreds of times before. About halfway home, there is a stretch of road with few lights and one could easily drive fast. Mario started revving up on me.

I'm thinking, "Alright, I'm not backing down from a challenge," so I rev back and take off.

It was late, so it was probably not a good idea to attract attention, but I guess we weren't thinking. We were racing down the street, but his heavy old truck was no match for my little Honda with a motor swap. I left him so far back, I couldn't even see him, so I eased off the gas to let him catch up.

The next thing I noticed was his big maroon colored Chevy truck pulling up on me, but he didn't slow down. He just flew past me and started veering off toward the right, and then I saw him slam straight into the metal traffic light pole.

"What the fuck?" are the words that came out of my mouth.

"Awe, he's going to be pissed, his truck is totaled," I thought to myself.

I drove past his truck and pulled off to the side. I put on my hazard signals and got out. I ran over to the truck and saw that the engine had small bursts of fire inside. As I ran up to the driver side and peeked through the shattered glass window I saw his body unconscious, slumped over the driver's steering wheel.

I thought, "Oh crap."

I grabbed the door handle to open it, but it wouldn't budge. It was pinned shut. I knew I had to get him out, so I hopped through the window with half my body dangling out and tried hauling his motionless body through the window. It was too tough. He was too much dead weight and the elevated angle made it seem impossible.

I started to think to myself, "What do I do?"

Just then a man walked up to me who had a cell phone up to his ear.

"The Paramedics and help are on the way," he said.

I was still trying to pull him out of the car 'cause I didn't know if the truck would catch fire. I guess I've watched it happen in too many movies.

Before I knew it an E.M.T (Emergency Medical Technician) grabbed my shoulder and said, "I will take it from here why don't you just go back to your car and sit tight."

I walked back to my car and I saw a fire truck and all sorts of people rushing over to help with Mario.

Just then I saw a police car and thought, "Shit I probably still have alcohol on my breath."

I got into my car and panicked, searching for anything I could find to mask the smell, just in case I had to talk to the police. All I could find was a cherry flavored Chap Stick in the center console. This would have to do.

I know, you're probably thinking "Chap Stick?"

I took the Chap Stick, rolled it down, and sank my teeth into the soft gushy substance. It was nasty, but there was no way I was getting a DUI. I was concentrating on chewing and spreading the Chap Stick all over the inside of my mouth.

The officer walked over to my car and started asking me questions. He asked me to step outside and talk to him and tell him what had happened. I was trying hard not to open my mouth too much and also not to directly look at him. He had me sit on the curb and asked me to call whomever I needed to and notify them that my brother would be going to the hospital. I told him I had no phone and he gave me his.

I dialed my mom, but was not expecting her to pick up, because it was like four in the morning. I was shocked to hear her voice after about the third ring.

"Hello?" she said.

"Miguel where are you?" she asked.

"The police just called and said you guys vandalized a gas station," she said.

Before she could finish with her story I interrupted with, "Mario just got in an accident. His car is totaled."

She said to put him on the phone and I told her, "No, I can't, he is passed out. You have to come down here. They're taking him to the hospital. Hold on, talk to the officer." I handed him the phone and they conversed.

CHAPTER 3

The Phone Call

All alone these subtle days are strangling me...
The walls are breathing and my mind unweaving...
I'm finding out things that I didn't know...
Counting the days till I surrender this ball and chain
and can have my peace of mind back...
When the darkness turns to light the déjà vu of
another Groundhog's Day will begin...
Every day for me now is Monday...
A dreary one, with not much to look forward to...

Miguel Scharmer

We were sleeping soundly when the phone rang at about 4:00 a.m. It was Miguel.

"Mario has been in a car accident," he said.

"What? Was he hurt? Did he total the truck?" I desperately asked.

Mario still owed us for the money we had loaned him to buy the truck and this was not the first time he had wrecked a vehicle.

Miguel said," You don't understand mom, he is hurt real bad."

Then a strange man got on the phone. "Is this Mrs. Scharmer?"

"Yes," I replied.

"This is the police. Your son is unconscious and has a heartbeat, but they are having trouble securing his airway. We don't know where we are taking him yet, but we will let you know as soon as we do. Stay where you are. Do not come down." the policeman stated.

We knew at that point just how serious the accident was. Mark and I had spent nine years on a search and rescue team. We were both trained in emergency medical response. We were concerned that the paramedics were not able to secure Mario's airway. Without enough oxygen he might die or suffer from traumatic brain injury. Where were they taking Mario, to the hospital or the morgue?

The crash was only two miles from our house. I have been told that most auto accidents happen near the home. This was certainly the case with our Mario.

Miguel drove to the house to get us. He had been in his own car following Mario home. Apparently Mario was drunk and had just finished dropping all the kids off. Brad had suggested that they spend the night at his house, but Mario didn't want to leave his truck parked out on the street.

In the movie *Sliding Doors*, there is a woman whose life unfolds in two completely different ways. In one scene she gets fired from her job and gets home just in time to find her boyfriend in bed with another woman. You can imagine how that story goes. In the other scenario, she gets fired, but misses the train home. The sliding doors of the train shut just as she is about to get on. She gets home late, giving her boyfriend plenty of time to get the lover out of the house, hide the evidence, and take a shower. In an instant one's life can change dramatically. People often beat themselves up by thinking, "If only I hadn't done this or had done that." Life happens and you never know what you are going to get.

CHAPTER 4

The Hospital

If I ever lose my faith in you, then I have lost my belief in the beauty of what lies beneath.
The bond from me to you can never be broken, torn or stolen.

Miguel Scharmer

Miguel arrived at the house and we all climbed into our car. We were anxious to get to the hospital. Miguel asked if we wanted to go by the wreck on the way. It was a minor detour. We both agreed to stop.

I was horrified to see what looked like a red soda can that someone had stepped on. The remains of Mario's truck were curled around a light post. The windshield was broken. Glass was spread all over the road and front seat of the truck. The keys were still in the ignition. The driver's seat was covered in blood. The back of the truck looked fine; the damage was to the front. The light post ran into the middle of the engine. How could anyone survive a crash like that? Fear gripped my body. The palms of my hands were wet with sweat. My stomach was in knots and my body started shaking.

"Oh my God! He has to live, please God let Mario be okay," I prayed.

The emergency room was crowded with people suffering from minor injuries to life threatening situations. Two police officers were hovering around waiting for the results of Mario's blood test. They wanted to know if he was under the influence of drugs or alcohol. We found out later that his alcohol blood level was .223!

After arriving at the hospital emergency room I decided to phone our good friend and neighbor Richard Carlson. It was 4:30 a.m., but he answered the phone! Richard was usually up at that time writing. He had always told us that the early morning hours were his best times to write. Richard wrote the *Don't Sweat the Small Stuff books*. When I told him what had happened to Mario, he said he would come right over to the hospital.

Mark and I decided not to call anyone else until we knew something more about Mario's condition. As Miguel paced, Mark sat and comforted me. I prayed, but couldn't stop my body from shaking. The not knowing would prove to be the hardest thing to endure during the entire hospital experience. We would be given hope one minute and news of doom the next.

After about an hour a doctor came out and told us they were stabilizing Mario. He had a broken femur, a cut hand, and a head injury. They would not know the extent of the head injury until they took a CAT scan. We could go in to see him shortly.

Richard arrived before we went in. He gave us hugs and support. Tears were in his eyes. He said he and Kris (Richard's wife) would be there for us. Richard gave us a spiritual picture, which we would end up keeping in Mario's room throughout the ordeal. That picture stayed in Mario's room for the next four years.

Richard Carlson died December 13, 2006, from a pulmonary embolism on a plane trip to New York. Upon Kris's request, I gave the picture back to her shortly after his death. The picture had now gone full circle.

After about an hour, but what seemed like an eternity, a doctor took us in to see Mario. When we arrived at his bed I was amazed. Mario looked like Sleeping Beauty. His face and body had hardly a scratch. He looked fine except for a laceration on his right hand and a splint on his right leg. How could anyone survive a crash like that and have so little damage? It was a miracle. He was unconscious and covered with wires which were hooked up to a heart monitor, a respirator and other life support machines. All the machines were just temporary emergency equipment and from the way he looked, I thought that Mario would be fine.

The emergency room doctor told us that Mario had sustained a traumatic brain injury and they wouldn't know the extent of the damage until they gave him a CAT scan. They were taking him in for an X-ray next. The doctor was amazed at how little external and internal damage was sustained after such a terrible crash. However, he was concerned about damage to Mario's brain.

I kissed Mario on the forehead and thanked God and the angels for saving his life. Little did I know that it would be twenty-one days before Mario would open his eyes. That would be followed by five grueling months of hospitals, intensive care units, a nursing home and a rehabilitation center before he came home. This was going to be an incredible life-changing experience for all of us.

CHAPTER 5

The First Seventy-Two Hours

If you open your locked door, the search for my ideals
remains no more...
Been through much pain and sorrow.
And you won't forget these words tomorrow.

Miguel Scharmer

We were put in a private waiting room where we sat exhausted and in
shock. It was about 9:00 a.m. before we got the results of the X-ray.
Mario had multiple bruising throughout his brain. His brain had been
rattled like bingo balls from the impact of the crash and had moved
inside the skull about four mm.

He had injury to his brain stem as well. Later we would discover
that the brain stem injury posed the biggest challenge to his survival.
The brain stem controls all the basic functions of the body, such as
heart rate and temperature. Mario would suffer from uncontrollable
fevers and rapid heart rate for months to come. The brain stem also
controls balance and motor skills, including speech.

Mario was given very strong drugs to keep him in an induced
comma. The drugs took Mario to the brink of death by minimizing
the brain's work, which allowed it to rest. Putting Mario into an
induced coma also kept the swelling down so his brain could begin to
heal. Swelling of the brain inside the skull posed the biggest danger
for Mario. In some cases surgery is necessary to release pressure. But
because Mario did not have a direct impact to any side of his head,
there wasn't a blood pool that surgery could release. Unlike our other
organs or muscles, the brain is enclosed in the skull and swelling can
create more damage to the tissue and even death. We were told that

after seventy-two hours, the worst of the swelling should peak so the doctors might have some idea of what to expect. It was possible that after the seventy-two hour window, Mario could wake up, talk and come home.

With this new information I now felt ready to call my parents and close friends. Mario would be fine; we just needed to wait out these first seventy-two hours.

When we told my parents, the first thing they wanted to know was what the doctors said. We explained to them the first seventy-two hour scenario, after which they said that they would be right over. My dad would take the bull by the horns and help keep us all focused. His sharp mind would be very useful in helping to get the many answers we needed.

My dad, Jim, is a very kind and loving man, but no one can stand in his way when he wants to get things done. He had worked with hospitals as an efficiency expert and that experience would prove to be another blessing for us when it came to navigating the hospital bureaucracy.

My mom, Bette, has a heart of gold. She is like the Divine Mother and I have always felt loved and safe with her. Like many mothers, she worries about all of her children and grandchildren. And because she is very sensitive, she can have nights of sleeplessness over the little things in life. I was concerned about what this might do to her.

My parents lived just a few blocks from the hospital, which was comfortingly convenient. When any of us got tired of hospital waiting rooms or uncomfortable chairs we could walk through a lovely park to their house.

After our talk on the phone my parents came right over. They too were amazed at how well Mario looked. We were all anxious for the seventy-two hour window to end, wanting this nightmare to be over so we could get back to living our lives.

My Flute

It was a cloudless, warm, summer day on August 9, 2002, and twenty-four hours had elapsed since the accident. The sunlight penetrated through the hospital curtains bringing us hope of sustained life. For me the waiting had become almost unbearable. I was tense and sleep deprived. My mom had given me an inspirational book to read, but I found it difficult to concentrate. I could only sit in the waiting room for one or two hours at a time without taking a break. Mark and I went on walks through the hospital and to my parent's house by the park. Getting in the fresh air and seeing some blue sky did wonders for my soul. We were never gone for more than an hour or so, just in case there was a change in Mario's condition.

Two people at a time could go in to see Mario, limited to ten minutes. If his brain pressure went up during our visit we were rushed out of the room. Sometimes when I visited Mario, I talked to him and put some holy ash on his forehead and in his mouth. Mario had a breathing tube down his throat and a feed tube up his nose. He had a cervical collar around his neck and was still covered with wires that were hooked up to various life support machines. What disturbed me the most was his right leg, which was in a cast and in traction. The doctors had drilled a hole into Mario's leg and had inserted a pin to keep the broken femur in place. To me it looked like something otherworldly, like a Frankenstein monster. Sometimes I would get light headed and feel like fainting when I looked at it.

How could this be happening to my son? I silently prayed again, asking God to please let him wake up so we could all go home and live our lives again.

While in the Intensive Care Unit (ICU) with Mario, I would whisper into his ear words of encouragement.

"Mario, you are relaxing your body and healing your brain. You are getting better and better every day in every way. We love you Mario and are here for you."

I composed a list of fifteen affirmations that I would read to Mario every day and have other visitors read to him too. It was important to me to not have anyone say something negative in front of Mario, even in his unconscious state.

I was well read in the area of near death experiences and knew that unconscious people could respond to outside stimulus. In many hospitals, relaxation and healing tapes were put on for patients before and after surgery to promote healing. I tried putting headphones on Mario with a healing tape, but when I did, his heart rate went up so high that we had to take them off. Maybe he couldn't stand the pressure of the headphones on his head. A smaller earphone, like the kind used with iPods, might have worked better, but I didn't think of that at the time.

After each visit, to help pull myself together, I went to the chapel in the hospital. This particular chapel had a beautiful stained glass window with a spiral of colors. I love spirals. There was also a book for people to write their prayers and thoughts in. It was very touching to read other peoples' experiences. By reading them I felt connected and not alone. Stuff does happen to others, I thought. Time and "normal life" had stopped for them too!

I found that playing my Native American song flute in the chapel increased my emotional well-being. As I played the flute my heart would go out to all the mothers of the Earth. I felt the pain of the mothers who had lost a child, husband, brother, sister, mother, or father. My heart would almost break with the weight of all this sorrow.

After about ten minutes of playing, I could play no more and just sat breathless, my nose running and my face wet with tears. Moments after I stopped playing a great peace engulfed me. I felt connected with the world. This was a huge emotional release for me. Full of gratitude, I sat and went to my heart center, listing in my mind all the things I was grateful for in my life.

Playing a wind instrument forces you to take deep breaths, this in turn helps you to relax. It is a very healing experience and I highly recommend it. You don't need to know how to read music to play a Native American flute; you just play from the heart.

I own three flutes but the one I played at the hospital was my favorite, and easiest for me to play. I had purchased this flute while on vacation in Sisters, Oregon, a month before Mario's accident! Did I buy the flute at that time for this reason?

It all began when Mark and I walked into a gift shop. I was drawn to that flute. It was a deep red color and said "Spirit" on its side. I asked if I could try it.

The shopkeeper said, "Sure go ahead."

I sang with that flute. My heart soared like the wings of an eagle. My husband pointed out that I already owned two other flutes, so we walked out of the store empty handed. The flute was $200, a lot of money for us at the time.

We continued to look around town some more, but the flute kept calling me. I had to buy that flute. I told my husband, I didn't know why, but I had to have it. Being the kind and gentle man that he is, he said, "Okay." One month later I would know why I had to have that flute.

CHAPTER 6

Helping Friends

I got hit in my head and slept in many areas that
made me realize the power of love. Now I know that
I can accomplish almost anything with love. Now I
am trying to spread my words of love. God put me
here to spread love and smile. Smiling feels good.

Mario

The first seventy-two hours were over now, so the primary neurosurgeon
came in to talk to us. He said that there had been very little change
in the swelling of Mario's brain. The brain pressure was still too high
to take him off the coma inducing drugs and it was too risky to do
any treatment on him at the time. They could not take care of the
broken femur or laceration on his hand until the pressure dropped.
All we could do was wait. The doctor told us that there was nothing
we could do.

"Go home and rest. We will call you if there is any change. You
may also call the hospital any time you want, to see how your son is
doing," he said.

My husband Mark had a business to run. We had two horses, two
dogs and seven chickens to take care of. I only had a few more weeks
before school started, so I could stay with Mario. We left the hospital
that evening wondering when the nightmare would end.

Mario and his brother were enrolled in massage school which was
scheduled to start in September. Surely Mario would be well enough
to go by then. We had already paid the two thousand dollar tuition
for the class.

Should I call the teacher just in case Mario couldn't make it?

Maybe I could get a refund back. At least Miguel could still go. It would be good for Miguel to have another focus. The accident had been very hard on him. I think he felt partly to blame, being his older brother.

I also had to cancel my school's staff party, which I was hosting at my house in two weeks.

We live in a beautiful house on a hill in Martinez, California, with a view of Mt. Diablo. We had just finished putting in a pool, patio deck, and peaceful serene landscaping. The yard was filled with meandering paths, rock walls, and flowering California native plants. I was eager to share its beauty with others.

The pool has a beach landing for easy access, gradually dropping from a few inches to seven feet at the deep end. We had two large statues of Sandhill Cranes mounted by a rock on the beach landing. I named one Happy and one Harmony.

It was time to cancel the party and let our extended family and friends know what had happened to our son. This was going to be tough. Mark and I wanted to keep a positive attitude. I was determined that Mario was going to make a 100% recovery.

Sharing with others was emotionally difficult, but we soon discovered people wanted to help. Since they couldn't come to the hospital, I delegated other jobs to family and friends. My older brother, Marc, became the communications expert. He kept family and friends informed of Mario's' status. We needed Marc to help us with the computer. At the time of Mario's crash we were not even online! Our computer was at least ten years old. I had never even sent an e-mail message. Marc got me the latest research on traumatic brain injury off his computer, which he printed out and mailed to me. I still have hundreds of sheets of information on the subject.

According to some neurologists, the progress you make in the first year is critical. One train of thought was that the brain is hardwired and that once injured cannot repair itself. After one year, very little improvement is expected. This was frightening information for us, especially with Mario taking so long to wake up.

New research is confirming that the brain has plasticity to it. The brain, if injured, finds new pathways to restore lost function. Other new research indicates that the brain can heal indefinitely. This was the belief that Mark and I embraced.

Some of my teaching buddies began making meals for us and brought them over every few days. It was difficult for me to eat, but I still had Mark and Miguel to feed. This was another wonderful act of kindness I would never forget.

Another friend helped with feeding our horses and chickens and dogs. We let the chickens out each day to scratch and roam in the yard. If you do not put them away by dusk, a hungry raccoon or coyote might take one for dinner.

I have explored various forms of healing for many years. Some of my interests were crystals, acupressure, massage, essential oils, acupuncture, sound, and hands-on healing. I had two friends that were very involved with giving healings. I called my friends Virginia and Nancy to help us. They frequently came to work on Mario. They were both allowed in the ICU because they were my spiritual ministers. Nancy and Virginia do hands-on healings and psychic readings.

We had two hundred and fifty poster photos of Mario from his completion of modeling school. I decided to start giving out Mario's pictures to people for prayers. We even put his handsome face in every hospital room he was in, so the nurses and doctors could connect with him as a special person and not just a broken body covered with wires, hooked up to life support.

Once my school started I developed a new routine. Every morning as soon as we got up, Mark would call the hospital. He got a report from the nurses to see if there were any changes in Mario's condition. If there was no change, Mark would go to his office first and then off to visit Mario later. After a quick protein drink, meditation, and Tai Chi, I would go to work. I wore cheerful colors, a smile on my face, and took my flute, so I could go and visit Mario right after school. This routine helped keep me sane for the next few months.

Mark gave me a cell phone so I could be on-call at any moment. I had never used a cell phone and had been critical of their use in public places. I found cell phones annoying, especially in movie theaters, restaurants, and cars.

"Why can't people wait until they get home to talk on the phone? Aren't answering machines good enough?" I often thought.

How judgmental I was about cell phones. In my life I have found that every time I make a critical remark about something, it comes right back to hit me in the face.

Another remark I would have to own up to was, "There are too many handicapped spaces in parking lots! It makes it so hard for me to find a space. Some of the people don't even look handicapped!" Now I complain that there are not enough disabled parking spots.

After teaching, I drove right to the hospital. It was about a thirty-minute drive. Once I got there, it was straight to ICU.

"Okay Chrissy, you can do this," I chanted to myself.

The nurses were informed of my presence and would let me in to see Mario, only if his vitals were stable enough. His brain pressure and heart rate were watched carefully.

Nurse Ann, who worked the first week with Mario in ICU, believed that Mario did respond to our visits. She told us not to listen to the dire predictions of the doctors and to never give up hope. She had seen many miracles in her career working at the hospital. We took her advice and were glad we did.

With my flute in hand I walked into the ICU and saw Mario. I held his hand and talked to him. I couldn't massage him because of all the wires, so I did a meditation and sent him love. I went to my heart center and visualized warm white healing light in and around Mario. I felt at peace while doing this. Deep in my heart I just knew Mario would be OK.

Whenever I visited Mario, his heart rate and brain pressure would go down. The nurses began to let me stay longer, even up to one hour at a time. I began to make friends with the nurses. They work so hard and have such stressful jobs. While the doctors prescribe drugs and treatment, it is up to the nurses to administer medications and watch the machines. I hardly ever saw a doctor, but I saw the nurses every day. My son's life was in their hands. I felt grateful for their service.

When nurses changed shifts, I offered neck and back massages to those leaving. I had studied massage and was quite good at giving them. In the elementary schools where I had worked, it was not unusual for me to give a neck and back release during recess or lunch to my fellow teachers. It felt good to give back a little something to these nurses who were keeping my son alive. I became very popular at the hospital. My massages were greatly appreciated and Mario became a sought-out patient because of them.

My husband learned how to read the machines so we could get

accurate feedback ourselves. We learned to use the machines as a communication device with Mario.

Did he like touch, music, or words spoken? Did some people upset him more than others? We would use his pulse oximeter to tell how he was responding to every visit each day. This machine measured his heart rate. When he was stressed, it would go up, when relaxed, down.

One evening, when my husband and I went to visit, we were not allowed to go into the ICU. The nurse told us that his sister was there. Sister? Mark and I looked at each other and thought: but Mario doesn't have a sister. After a short time a beautiful blond teenage girl came out. Her name was Gina and she was one of "Mario's girls." She went to school with Mario and had dated him. She found out about the accident at school. The crash had been printed in the school paper and Gina wanted to see Mario so badly that she had lied about being his sister. Gina came to see Mario every day. She had so much love and dedication to him that we never did tell the nurses that she was not his sister. Another "sister" of Mario's was Ana. She too lied about her relationship to Mario so she could get in to see him.

Mario's condition changed slowly. The brain pressure was still too great to take him off the coma inducing-drugs. Sometimes days would pass before we saw the neurologist responsible for Mario's care.

Friends and family were all asking, "How is Mario? What does the doctor say?" We didn't have any answers.

On my father's advice, we left the doctor multiple messages, but still received no response. Having worked in hospitals as a management engineer, my father was determined to see the doctor. On one occasion he called and talked to the doctor's office assistant. She said the doctor was very busy and scheduled for surgery at the hospital in an hour. She promised to give the doctor the message that my dad had called.

My dad didn't wait for a return phone call. Instead he parked himself in front of the door where the surgery was being performed and waited. When the doctor came out of surgery, there was my dad. The doctor didn't say much to him. He was irritated, but did call us with a report on Mario's status that day. No change yet. He said he would schedule a family meeting to talk with us in more detail, but to please tell my dad not to bug him in the hallways.

The doctor said, "Write down any questions you might have." A few days later we got our meeting.

We all sat at a round table; my father, my husband, the doctor, and myself. We had many questions:

How long was Mario to be kept in a coma?

Would brain surgery release the pressure?

When would they fix his leg?

Was Mario his worst case?

What were his chances of recovery?

The doctor told us that they would keep Mario in an induced coma until his brain pressure was down to a safe level. If they took the drugs away too early, he could sustain even more brain damage. He also said that his leg was the least of his worries and could be repaired later without complications to it. He said that the longest case of an induced coma he had experienced was for an Olympic athlete at Lake Placid New York. A young woman hit a tree at sixty miles per hour while snow skiing. She was kept in a coma for three weeks. She didn't die, but he wasn't sure about the details of her recovery. He did tell us not to give up hope, but if Mario survived the coma, we should expect a long rehabilitation.

"It would be like starting over with a suckling baby," the doctor told us.

He also said not to be afraid of our Health Maintenance Organization's rehabilitation facility. He said that it was a state of the art rehabilitation center.

Wow, I felt like a bomb had been dropped.

"Starting over, like a baby." My mind kept repeating the words.

"Now what?" I thought.

Being a school teacher, I decided to get started. I could do this. I shouldn't wait for Mario to wake up. His brain would need stimulation as soon as the doctor felt it was safe. The doctor told me we could try some sensory stimulation, as long as his brain pressure stayed at a reasonable level.

It seemed like my entire life training and experience had all become skills given to me to help with Mario's recovery. Having been a special education teacher for severely behavior-disordered children would be very useful in handling the rages we would encounter later. The kindergarten teaching experience gave me the skills for organizing the sensory training Mario would need.

Knowing how to delegate jobs would prove to be essential in organizing all the family and friends that would help with the rehabilitation of Mario while he was in the hospital. Even having been a mother was useful with toilet training Mario and teaching him to crawl, eat, and walk again. We were really going to have to raise Mario twice. The second time around would not only take longer, but would be much more intense.

I put together a sensory awareness training kit which would help to begin awakening Mario's senses. Sight was out, because Mario's eyes were still closed and would not be open for many weeks, but smell, taste, touch, and sound were available.

To stimulate touch, I collected various items with different textures. I started with rabbit fur, silk, feather, sandpaper, cotton, a pinecone and other various items. I gently rubbed these against Mario's skin. Mario's brain pressure would go down a little with the soft objects like feathers, fur, and silk. The pressure would go up with sandpaper. Mario seemed to especially like the inside of his arms lightly touched with a feather.

For smell, I used cotton swabs dipped in spices or essential oils. These included lavender, lemon, cinnamon, clove, dill, allspice, vinegar, bitter chocolate, eucalyptus, and frankincense.

To awaken taste I wanted to cover sweet, salt, sour, and bitter. I would put a drop of the material on the cotton swab and then under Mario's nose for smell and all around the tongue for taste. Different parts of the tongue taste the different flavors. Mark and I would watch the monitors for a response. We got a reaction after each stimulation. If his pressures would go up a little, we would stop so we would not over-stimulate his brain.

Mario couldn't tolerate much sound, but if I picked very soft, soothing music or relaxation tapes, his brain pressure would go down. We still could not use headphones or an earphone without agitating him. I kept a CD player in Mario's room and we played soft music while we visited. The nurses liked the music as long as it seemed to calm Mario. They also put music on for Mario when they were alone with him. Time passed and I wondered how long it would be before Mario would wake up?

CHAPTER 7

The Awakening

Forget what we're told.
Erase what's been branded in our minds.
Live for the moment,
For each second that passes is a memory
We will never be able to duplicate or get back.

Miguel Scharmer

Days turned into weeks. It would be Mario's birthday in a few days. Would I get to see his beautiful brown eyes by then? He would turn nineteen August 31, 2002. School would start after Labor Day and I needed to get my classroom ready and attend faculty meetings. Please Mario, wake up!

By now we had met an entire crew of "Mario's girls." They were all cute and wanted desperately to see Mario. They all asked why Gina could go in but not them? I had to tell the girls that the nurses thought Gina was his sister and thus a family member. I was not about to lie and create a gang of sisters.

Many of the girls didn't know each other and this created tension. As previously mentioned, Mario had been quite the ladies' man. I only knew three girls out of the entire group. They were all eighteen or nineteen. We met Gina, Nicole, Stephanie, Ana, Jenell, Rochelle, Zaina, and Chrissy the first few weeks after the accident.

I took everyone's name and number. Later, when Mario was awake and out of the intensive care unit, I would schedule visits for all of Mario's friends, using a weekly calendar to keep everything organized. I scheduled hourly visits, but no more than five a day. Visitors were given instructions not to stay more than one hour, so Mario would not get over stimulated.

I asked visitors not to wake Mario up when he was sleeping. I kept a journal in the room for them to write his vitals down and what they did for Mario. I trained them to do range of motion exercises, massage, and sensory stimulation with the kits I had made. They could also read to him. I composed a list of fifteen positive affirmations that were available to read to Mario each day. I posted a daily schedule on a white board in his room. The schedule let the nursing staff know who was coming and when. Each visitor knew who was next to arrive and I told him or her how important it was to honor the scheduled visiting time. I asked visitors to be punctual and leave when the next person arrived. All of this visiting took place after Mario was awake and out of the ICU. I believe that it was our efforts and the love of his family and friends that kept Mario alive. If Mark and I had tried to do it all ourselves without their help, he might not have survived.

The hospital was very limited as to what they were able to provide for Mario, especially after he got out of the ICU. They knew Mario needed range of motion, but rarely gave it to him. He was lucky if he got twenty minutes a day. By training extended family and friends, we got Mario twenty minutes of range of motion (R.O.M.) four of five times a day.

If the body is not moved consistently, recovery can be impaired. If you don't use it, you lose it. That's why everything we did with sensory stimulation and range of motion was so important.

August 31, 2002. Mario's birthday! I called the hospital in the morning to see how Mario was doing. The doctor was reducing the coma-inducing drugs because the brain pressure had dropped. The nurses were waiting to see if they got any response from him. This was exciting news. Maybe I would get to see Mario open his eyes. He might even move a hand or foot. What a beautiful birthday gift it would be to have Mario back. Since it was Mario's birthday, Mark and Miguel both came with me

"Please God wake Mario up!" I thought out loud to myself.

As we drove to the hospital I noticed what a bright, warm, summer day it was. The sky was clear and blue. We were all very anxious to get to the hospital to see Mario. After parking the car, we rushed up to the third floor and went into Mario's room. His eyes were open! He was staring blankly up at the wall. I hugged him and wished him a happy birthday. He did not respond. Couldn't he hear me? Mark and Miguel both talked to Mario but no response. We were all crushed. Was this our new Mario, like a vegetable, unresponsive to anyone? No, I refused to give up. It had to be the drugs. He would get better.

After a good cry I went to the chapel to compose myself.

At the chapel I remembered what my friend Nancy had said: "Mario will recover, but it will take a long time."

I could do this. Maybe it would be a couple of years, but Mario was young. He would only be twenty-one in two years and could still have a full and productive life. I convinced myself. For some reason I had a two-year recovery plan stuck in my head. In the meantime, I needed to continue with my life. I had a classroom to set up and students to teach.

I have always been a very dedicated teacher and hard worker. I usually started working in my classroom weeks before school was in session. There were only a few days left, so how was I going to get ready on time? I called in the troops. Most of the people I called had been parents of previous students that I had taught and had made friends with. I also got help from some close friends.

I made lists of the things that needed to be done, and like magic; everything was in order before the first day of school. Never had I set up a classroom so quickly and efficiently. One of my new parents did all my class lists, field trip notes, and "Back to School Night" handouts. She did everything I needed that required a computer. I was slow to enter the "computer age" and now wasn't a good time to learn something new. I was on overload as it was. Pat, who had a wonderful spirit, would do all my computer work over the next five years until I retired!

At "Back to School Night" I had everyone in tears when I shared our nightmare and asked for help with the classroom. I had a huge list of volunteers that year.

It didn't take long for me to realize that the universe provides everything that you need, but you have to ask and be ready to receive. One of my favorite affirmations is this: **I deserve everything that the universe has to offer me and I choose to receive it now.**

School started and my new attire included a fanny pack with cell phone. I was on-call 24/7. My principal was very supportive and didn't complain when I had to leave a faculty meeting to answer my cell phone. My students got quite good at getting instantly quiet when a call came in. I didn't hide the situation of Mario's crisis from them or their parents.

At first, Mark and I were not sure if we should share the truth of Mario driving under the influence. After some time we decided that honesty was the best policy. Maybe by telling the truth it might change someone's decision to drink and drive. This tragedy could be a powerful tool even for eight-year olds.

That first year after the crash, I brought in pictures of Mario and told stories about his hospital stay and recovery. I shared these pictures at lunchtime in the staff room. How frightening those pictures must have been for the faculty to see. Mario's progress was slow and he didn't look like the young model they all knew. Many of the staff had children and didn't want to think such a tragedy could happen to their child: who would? My head was in the clouds and I had so much hope that each little improvement was a milestone.

"Mario sat up today in a chair for ten minutes," remembering how thankful I was when it happened.

"Mario turned his head to the left," another incredible step.

I was like a new mother, thrilled at her baby's first bite of solid food, or first step.

Everyone kept asking me, "Has he talked yet? What do the doctors say? When can he come home?"

I had no answers to any of those questions.

CHAPTER 8

The Move

How is it that one can feel so down and lost when the world around sees him as one of the happiest people to be around?

Look close... Even closer... Take the time and depth to see what makes this person... They're are millions of faces in the world and we walk by and glance at them through car windows... on BART... across the room while dining...

The world can look like the happiest place...

One can, and often will, try to profile another in a glance...

Doing a quick financial scan of the individual...

This is still a material world we live in...

It doesn't mater how rich you are... where you're from...

who went to college... who was on honor roll...

Every family has its problems and always will...

We as people are built imperfect and if nothing hard has ever come for you, in your life,

I feel sorry for you...

Because only through our hardships can we truly learn, and find out who we really are and the depth of who the people around us are...

I have lived a very colorful, eventful life, but you may never guess it by just a glance...

You have to dig a bit deeper...

Miguel Scharmer

Mario's doctor met with us again on our next visit to the hospital. He told us that our HMO was anxious to move Mario to their facility. Mario's doctor didn't want to move him yet. He said he would do what he could to keep him where he was until his broken femur was repaired. The doctor also explained to us that it was time to put a feeding tube in Mario's stomach and a tracheotomy for breathing. It had been over twenty days and Mario would be more comfortable without the tubes in his nose and throat. Both were simple operations and would not cause Mario undue stress. We agreed to have the surgery, which was scheduled for the following day.

That night I had a terrible time sleeping. I was afraid that Mario's beautiful body would be scarred forever. I envisioned him with a hole in his neck and the scar he would keep forever. When I finally fell asleep I saw Mario in a dream.

He told me over and over, "Don't let them cut my neck mom, I will be fine. I don't need the tracheotomy, I can breathe on my own."

I woke up with a start. I told my husband about the dream. He said Mario needed the surgery and that I shouldn't worry. It was just a dream. All day I was bothered and stressed by my dream. I called my friends Virginia and Nancy. They both said to go ahead with the surgery. I relented. After all, it was only a dream.

I had other dreams about Mario. In one dream I saw him walking down a hallway with a cane and a limp. He was no longer the handsome boy I had known, but broken, his body distorted and deformed. With the end of each dream, I was beginning to realize that Mario's recovery was not only going to take a long time, but that he would never be the same. How could anyone be the same after such a devastating accident? We really had lost a son, our youngest, that we had so lovingly raised for eighteen years. It was depressing to think of all the time, energy, and love that we had put into Mario the first time. Now all of that seemed wasted and lost.

After the surgery Mark and I went to see Mario. I was horrified to see him with a tracheostomy tube in his neck. Now it was clear that Mario's recovery would be slow, but how slow?

Mario still needed one more operation before he was moved: his femur repair. The day before his scheduled surgery we got a call from our HMO. They were going to move Mario at once, even before having his leg repaired. I called Mario's doctor, but he said that he couldn't keep Mario any longer--that it was now safe to move him. His leg would have to wait until he was in the new hospital. I said goodbye to all the nurses, with tears in my eyes. They had saved Mario's life and I was grateful. Would our new hospital do as well? I could only hope and pray that everything would be OK.

Gina and her sister Nicole came to help us with Mario's things. He had a CD player, his sensory kit, some creams, many stuffed animals, and tons of flowers, pictures and cards. I told Mario that he was moving to another hospital and that everything would be fine. He did not respond. He just kept staring at the wall. After all the papers had been signed, the ambulance transport came. Three strong men came in to move Mario. They were concerned about his leg being in traction. They would have to take it out of the hospital's traction and put it in a temporary portable one. It was not an easy thing to do. They disconnected many of the wires and hooked them up to portable machines. I asked if I could ride with Mario in the ambulance and they said I could. This would be the first of many rides to come. I held Mario's hand and stroked his hair.

It seemed that Mario had made the transfer well. When we got to our hospital he was moved to the third floor ICU. To my surprise the nurse that received him was a former parent of a student I had taught the year before. What a miracle. She was happy to see me, but so sorry that my son was badly injured. She told me not to give up hope. She too, like Ann, our other nurse, had seen many miracles.

We got Mario comfortable and left for the night. All was not well. During the night Mario's brain pressure had gone way up and he had a 102 fever with a rapid heart rate. What was wrong? He had been fine before the move. The hospital called us in the morning to let us know about the change in his condition. They were doing everything they could to try and stabilize Mario. We both had to go to work. I would go in to see Mario that evening. Mark would go in the morning just as soon as he could.

All day long I worried about Mario. I called my parents and asked them to check on Mario, which they did. Everyone was worried and concerned.

During lunch I called my friends Virginia and Nancy. Nancy said she would go to the hospital and do a healing on Mario. That made me feel better. I kept my faith and prayed that Mario would be all right. Virginia couldn't go to the hospital that day, but did do a psychic reading and healing from home. She told me that the jury was still out in regards to whether Mario was going to return to his body and live with us or move on into the light.

I have talked to Mario about his out-of-body experiences, and this is what he told me: "When I died, three angels came for me. One had long white hair and shined all white like a beautiful lady. Her name was Naomi. The other was a bald man all in white. The third was just light. The angels wanted me to go with them, but I felt my mom's love and wanted to return to my body. I came back not for my dad, brother, grandma or grandpa. I came back for my mom. She and I are one."

I refused to give up hope. I kept telling Mario to live. I prayed to God and the angels for his recovery. Nancy told me that Mario would recover, but it would take a long time. What was a long time? One year, two years, or more?

During this critical time in the ICU, I began giving out more poster shots of Mario, asking people to pray for him. I had entire church congregations praying for Mario. Catholics, Protestants, Hindus, and Jews were all praying for Mario. I believe today that it was this powerful love force that kept Mario with us on this Earth plane. It has not been easy taking care of him, but it has been a great adventure and I am grateful for his decision to stay with us.

I read an article on the front page of the newspaper about the power of prayer: "Is Faith a Wonder Drug?" It said that scientists at such prestigious institutions as California Pacific Medical Center in San Francisco, Duke University in North Carolina, and George Washington University's Institute for Spirituality and Health in Washington D.C., are exploring the relationship between healing and prayer. Scientists say prayer can influence a patient's healing, but why it works remains a mystery.

CHAPTER 9

Roller Coaster Ride from Hell

This could be Heaven or this could be Hell.
Hard to distinguish this tangled web of a world that
is weaved.
Drink to celebrate or to forget.
Darkest hour to the brightest day!

Miguel Scharmer

The next five weeks would be like a roller coaster ride. On some days, Mario would seem stable and ready to receive his much needed leg surgery, but then at other times, he would get a fever, develop a high heart rate and increased brain pressure. What was going on? During this entire vacillating period a neurologist never talked to us. The floor doctors and nurses were our only hospital sources of information, and they didn't know what the problem was. How I wanted to bundle Mario up and take him back to the trauma center that had saved his life. Our insurance company would not allow us to do so.

When Mario was stressed he looked to us like he was in pain. His face would be contorted with a wrinkled brow. His mouth would sometimes be open like someone screaming, but no sound came out.

We asked the doctors if indeed he was in pain, but they said, "It is just his brain injury."

On one occasion my husband Mark asked if maybe his leg was hurting him, but they replied, "No, it is in traction so everything should be just fine."

One day, when we arrived after work to see Mario, I put on peaceful music, dimmed the lights and massaged him. After about an hour his heart rate dropped. It felt good to see Mario relaxed. I was ready to go home and get some sleep myself.

Just as I started to leave, a nurse's aide came in to change the sheets. I asked her to please come back later, that I had just gotten my son comfortable and sleeping. She said she had to do it now! My husband and I watched helplessly as the woman rolled Mario on his side and began to strip the bed. This was not an easy task with one leg in traction so I helped her.

Almost immediately Mario's heart rate and brain pressure went up. I felt like crying or screaming. My poor son was uncomfortable again, but I was too tired to do another massage. We stayed for one more hour and left around 11:00 p.m. knowing that Mario was agitated and uncomfortable. I went home that night and cried myself to sleep.

Since Mario responded so well to my voice, I decided to tape record it saying affirmations. The nurses could play the tape for him if he was having a bad day.

Nancy had loaned me a tape that had the human heart beating at rest. She thought the rhythmic beat might help him to control his own heart rate, perhaps by matching the rhythm that he heard with his own. It worked!

After about five weeks of the roller coaster ride, Mario stabilized. The doctors now felt he could survive the surgery for his broken femur. His surgery was scheduled in five days' time.

CHAPTER 10

Surgery

Love is the one thing that everyone can do and is very powerful.
With love you can accomplish a lot.
Love is the only element that you have that no one can copy.

Mario

September 14th was a beautiful, clear, fall day. We were anxious to speak to the Doctor about Mario's leg surgery. Mario was in the preoperational room. I had prepared myself with prayers and a meditation that morning. Mark was there to hold my hand and my brother came to the hospital for moral support.

This surgery was very important to us because Mario had always been athletic and we were expecting a full recovery. Mario loved to snowboard and had just received a new board on Christmas Day. How could he snowboard with only one good leg?

The reality was that his leg was the least of his problems. Even with perfect bones and muscle, his brain could not control his movements to walk, let alone snowboard. Today, after seven years, we are still working toward getting Mario to walk independently. It is our hope that keeps us going. I am grateful for the hope and faith I had during these difficult times.

Mario went in for the surgery around 8:00 a.m. We stayed in the hospital waiting room for an hour before I got anxious. Mark decided I needed to go on a walk around town. He found it very helpful to move during uncomfortable emotional situations that you have no control over. Sometimes moving is a better meditation than sitting. Trying to force yourself to relax just doesn't always work. The walking helped me a lot. After an hour of walking, we returned to the hospital waiting room. Mario was still in surgery. It was 11:00 a.m. What was taking so long?

Three hours later the doctor finally came out to talk to us. He was sweating profusely and looked like he had just finished a ten-mile marathon run. He said the surgery had been successful. The leg should heal nicely, but infection was always a risk after surgery. If he didn't get an infection, everything should be fine. It seems comical now, but we did ask the doctor if Mario would be able to snowboard with his newly repaired leg. He said the leg should not be a problem for him.

The reason why the operation had taken so long was because the broken femur had mended itself incorrectly. New bone had fused the two broken pieces together, but they were not in alignment.

"The leg was in traction. So why were they not aligned properly?" I asked.

The doctor didn't know.

We were pretty sure we knew the answer. It must have been the move from one hospital to the other. It probably happened when the transport people had to have his leg put into a temporary traction for the ambulance drive!

Maybe it had come out of traction and the bones had moved. His leg should have been X-rayed again at that point. We had asked before if that might have been the cause of Mario's agitated state and increased brain pressure on his first night after the move. Why hadn't anyone listened to our concerns? Mario had been in pain for two weeks with no way to tell anyone the source of his pain. Poor Mario.

Mark and I were angry. Should we hire a lawyer and sue our hospital for their error? We thought about it, but we just didn't have the time or energy it would take to proceed. We were drained and needed to conserve every ounce of energy for Mario. We put the notion of a lawsuit on the back burner and focused our attention on getting Mario up and running again.

Mario will be living the rest of his life with a nine-inch rod in his leg. We asked the doctor if metal detectors would register this at airports and security checks. He said no.

Mario spent one more day in the ICU recovering from his surgery and then he was moved to a regular bed on the respiratory ward. He shared a room and it was therefore difficult to do the healings, massage range of motion (ROM) and sensory training without disturbing the other patients.

To keep his new roommates happy I made sure to introduce myself, explain the situation, and offer a healing massage to him or her. All of the patients were receptive. None of them had the stream of visitors that Mario did. They were starving for attention and I could fill some of their needs. What first had seemed like a problem was quickly resolved.

Now that the surgery was over I thought it would be smooth sailing, but it was not to be. Mario continued to have high heart rates, along with sweats and fevers, for the next month. Every day the nurses would take blood to find the source of his "infection." Poor Mario became a human pincushion with all the drawing of blood and injecting of medications. A special line was inserted surgically to make it easier to administer his medications.

The journal I kept in his room during these times confirms just how desperate the situation was with his high heart rate and fevers.

I regularly reviewed the journal, and began to see patterns developing in Mario's physiology. When his friends and family first arrived in the room, his heart rate would be high, 115 to 160 beats per minute (bpm). By the time they left, it would drop, sometimes to as low as 72 bpm. The average person's heart rate at rest is between 60 and 80 bpm.

Another observation I made was his responsiveness. The doctors and neurologists said Mario was in a persistent vegetative state with failure to respond. This was not the case with family and friends. Visitors recorded many times that Mario had squeezed their hand. Sometimes he even smiled when given a lollipop to taste.

When one of the nurses brushed his teeth, he would follow her commands to open and shut his mouth. Once, when a girlfriend came to visit, he cried tears. These responses showed us that Mario was not in a vegetative state, but how could we prove this to the doctors? Mario cried many times that first year, but not since. He says that when his heart feels sad, he wants to cry, but his eyes will not tear. We do not know why.

CHAPTER 11

Training the Troops

Take a picture, take my picture, take your picture, take his picture, take her picture, life is one big roll of film and you are the photographer... no memory or event is too small and it's not always the biggest most important events in our lives that stand out in our minds... It's the small things that make you smile or the song that brings you back to a place you will never be again, but reminisce with... Experiences good or bad will help you understand and grow to a higher learning... Pay attention to the people in your life that will stick by your side and those who can forgive... Give to someone less fortunate... Charity with no sense of return is a true selfless act, whether the man upstairs is paying attention or not... Live each day not as it was your last, but that does not mean you should not live your present life to the fullest... I'm not talking about money... fancy cars... or a big home... do what truly matters to you... remember materials come and go, but memories can last forever and as they say, heroes are remembered and legends never die...

Miguel Scharmer

As I've already mentioned, when Mario was first injured, many people called and wanted to know what they could do to help. At the time all we needed was their love and prayers, but I had kept in mind that these wonderful friends and family could be very helpful later. Now it was time to call in the troops.

Nurse Solon, a male nurse who befriended Mario, was adamant that he get into a rehabilitation program, but how? The doctors at the hospital would not send him until they felt he was ready to benefit from therapy. He had to be able to respond to commands and show that he was not in a vegetative state. Mario was responding to family, nurses and friends, but not the doctors. Part of the problem was that the doctors spent so little time with Mario. Each doctor's visit was at most ten minutes and not even every day. With our one to two hour visits, Mario had more time to respond.

The hospital itself was not set up for therapy. Mario needed range of motion exercise (ROM) several times each day. His arms, legs, hands and feet were massaged and moved in special ways. The physical therapist would only come in a couple of times a week. Because of our concerns and wanting more R.O.M., she offered to train my husband and me in what to do. It was time-consuming and took about a half an hour or more to range him.

Mario didn't like us to manipulate his right arm, which was bent and held close to his chest in a clenched fist. You had to pry his arm open, and sometimes he resisted. His brain was contracting the entire right side of his body. When we did R.O.M., his heart rate would usually go way up. This was an indication we were upsetting him or causing pain, but it had to be done.

As working parents, it was too much for us to give Mario all the therapy he needed. In addition to R.O.M., we were giving massages, using the sensory kit, reading affirmations, and doing hands-on healing. We needed help. Because of my schoolteacher experience I knew just what to do.

I decided to train family and friends at a two hour workshop on how to care for Mario. I called my friend Nancy and made arrangements to use her center, "The Life Knowledge Center," for the class. It had a nice open room and was centrally located, which made it easily accessible for everyone. I invited about twenty people, but only ten were able to come. It was enough. Mario's grandparents came, along with his aunt and uncle, his brother Miguel, and many girlfriends.

At the training I put up chart paper and explained the routine. When they first arrived in the hospital room they were to look at the dry-erase board containing a schedule. Everyone could see who had been there last. Then they needed to sign in and read the journal to see what therapy had been given last. Mario's heart rate and temperature were to be recorded too. After that they could proceed with one of the therapies.

I taught them how to use the sensory kit and massage his hands and feet. I demonstrated how to give range of motion. We paired up and practiced on each other. After the practice I passed around a calendar and arranged for everyone to visit for one-hour intervals on specific days each week. I wanted Mario to have no more than five visits a day from morning to evening. There were enough people to give Mario R.O.M., massage, sensory stimulation, and a hands-on healing every day.

We started this program on September 18th and continued it until he went to the rehabilitation center in mid-December. I will be eternally grateful to all the wonderful people who shared their time and love with Mario.

The hospital staff had never seen anything like this before. They were cooperative when I explained the program and they let us proceed with the visits, even though they were not always during visiting hours. They would look at the schedule and try not to interrupt, especially if Mario was receiving a professional massage or hands-on healing.

One nurse was quite upset when a bottle of frankincense broke, sending a cloud of fumes clear down into the nursing station. I was a little upset too, considering the bottle cost one hundred dollars!

The training that I gave everyone was a Godsend. I would recommend doing it if you have someone who cannot communicate, is suffering, or in need of constant attention. Most hospitals and especially nursing homes do not have the time or staff to give such patients the care they need. Many people feel awkward in hospitals and nursing homes and really don't know what to do, so they avoid going. Giving people the tools they need is a winning situation for everyone.

With all this time, energy and love, how could Mario not get better?

CHAPTER 12

I Won't Go There

The one thing that keeps me going is my love for myself and my family. My angels also keep me from leaving. They kept me from leaving during the crash and after the crash by holding onto me.

Mario

How did we survive such travail during this ordeal? The hospital doctors were not optimistic. They would not recommend a rehabilitation facility. In fact they were making arrangements for Mario to be transferred to a skilled nursing home in the area. They were having trouble finding one equipped to handle Mario's needs. We were concerned about another move, especially since he continued to have high heart rates and fevers. The stress of the situation could have driven us mad.

Our close friend and neighbor Richard Carlson was talking over the fence to my husband Mark and he asked what had enabled us to keep so strong and wise during this entire experience.

Mark told him with a smile, "Four simple words: 'I won't go there.' Truthfully, that's our secret. We simply don't allow ourselves to go down that path of worry and dread. Since the situation is tough enough, allowing our minds to take us to even more difficult scenarios would make life almost unbearable."

So we took the move to a nursing home in stride, convinced that it would only be a stepping stone to a rehabilitation facility. Moving day came on Saturday October 26th. We were told that Mario was going to get a private room.

It turned out that he was a carrier of a type of staph bacteria. He did not have an infection himself, but could infect other people. All his fevers were not from an infection, but were caused from his brain stem injury. He had " brain fever." His high heart rate too was caused from his brain stem injury.

We were happy to be leaving the hospital and hoped that a private room with lots of rest and tender loving care would be just what Mario needed.

When the hospital nurse told us that they would not be sending a pulse oximeter to his new home we were horrified.

"What do you mean he doesn't need one? That machine is the only way we have of communicating with Mario," I protested.

Our health maintenance organization (HMO) was not going to pay for a machine that the patient didn't require for life support. Mario had improved enough that he was not a high risk for a cardiac arrest, so our request for the machine was denied.

Mark and I would not take no for an answer. After a lot of questioning, we discovered that there were places we could rent the machine for $300 a month. The papers were filled out and arrangements were made to get the machine delivered to the nursing home before Mario arrived.

The room in which Mario was placed was quite large and set up to hold three patients! We had the entire room to ourselves. It was dirty when we saw it, but the manager of the home assured us that it would be thoroughly cleaned before Mario arrived.

This was great. Because of his "infection" which was causing Mario no harm, we were getting a private room!

It was not easy to move Mario. He had accumulated a lot of stuff. Fortunately Gina and Nicole, the twins, were there to help. They carried toys, pictures, the boom box, CD's, massage oils, healing rocks, the sensory kit, dry erase board, my journal, and books. Again I rode with Mario in an ambulance.

The guys who came to transport Mario were the same ones who had moved Mario from one hospital to the other. They were cheerful and happy to see Mario's improvement. I told them that this move was temporary, no longer than a hundred days. It was just a pit stop on the way to a rehabilitation facility.

It is not uncommon to send traumatic brain injured (TBI) patients to a nursing home before going to a rehabilitation facility. It can be a good thing if you find the right home, because it provides more time for healing before the intense work of a rehabilitation program. Finding a good place is the challenge.

Some nursing homes are under-staffed and are more like warehouses, storing unwanted elderly patients who are at the end of their lives. Many patients have been abandoned by family and friends and sit in wheel chairs with blank, hopeless and helpless looks on their faces. We did not want Mario to go to a place like that.

When I taught kindergarten, I took my students once a month to visit nursing homes, to spread love to the patients. I taught the children not to fear the elderly and sick. Our visits brought a lot of love to the patients. Many looked forward to our monthly visits with anticipation. Now my young son was going into one. I never would have dreamt it possible.

Mario was the square peg in the round hole. He was the only young patient in the home with a tracheostomy (the director assured us they had dealt with them before) and he was also the most severely disabled.

We arrived shortly after eleven on a Saturday morning. The room had not been cleaned and the nurse on duty didn't seem to know what was going on. They were short-handed on the weekend and what had looked like a top-notch facility during the week looked neglected and dirty on the weekend. What was it going to be like here?

Before we left the hospital that morning, some of Mario's nurse friends had warned us to keep a close eye on Mario while at this home. They had heard bad reports about the care, or lack of care, at this facility.

Mario was moved to a bed and his feeding tube was hooked up. He was on a constant feed. He had an oxygen bottle attached to his tracheostomy tube. We were happy the pulse oximeter was in place and explained to the head nurse how we used it to communicate with Mario. If he had a high heart rate he was stressed and they should check his temperature, comfort him, and call us if it stayed elevated for more than an hour.

His medications did not arrive until six that evening. By then Mario was getting very stressed.

In hindsight I would suggest never moving a patient on the weekend. It did not go smoothly. We picked a Saturday so we wouldn't have to miss more work. Some homes are short handed on weekends, so it is not a good time to move a new patient in.

By 8:00 p.m. the medications had kicked in. We had Mario all tucked into bed and were ready to go home. I gave him a kiss and prayed that all would be well, but it was not to be. What followed was a continuous stream of small disasters, requiring our constant vigil to insure Mario's safety.

CHAPTER 13

I Am Not a Carrot

My dreams torture my reality... I dream I am a fish swimming upstream against a current that wants to push me ashore and out to dry... Let me find my way to the ocean... I want to fly through the stream into the world, submerged effortlessly through nets, which may try to keep me off course from reaching my purpose... Cast your reel if you wish, but I will not be lured or tempted to fall off course, for my Pisces is waiting for me at the end of the stream to take me home...

Miguel Scharmer

Now, we joke about Mario being called a vegetable. "What kind of vegetable are you Mario? A carrot, zucchini, cabbage, lettuce?"

Mario says, "No, no, no, I am celery."

Seven years ago it was no laughing matter. The doctors were not trying to be cruel or heartless with their evaluations, but that is how it felt. They were speaking from their truth and background of experience.

Most people with an injury like Mario's don't survive, let alone get much better. The heart usually gives out from all the stress, or they die from infections and fevers. The doctor's opinions were understandable. However, we did not choose to embrace them. What was not acceptable was the negative, heartless talk we experienced at the nursing home from one of the staff's physical therapists.

On Monday, Mark and I returned to the nursing home to meet with the director and visit with Mario. I went right to the director's office to see if she was in. She was there and I expressed my concerns over the dirty room. She apologized and commented that they were short-handed on the weekend, but would make sure the room was immediately cleaned. We looked at our calendars and scheduled an appointment to meet with everyone who would be working with Mario: the physical therapist, the speech therapist, the occupational therapist, and the nurse.

At this meeting, a therapy program would be planned with goals and objectives set up in writing. That sounded great and I left the room happy and relieved. This place just might work out after all. Unlike the hospital, they were creating a plan of action. Then I saw Mark in the hallway. He did not look happy.

My husband told me, "You will not believe what just happened. When I went into the room to visit with Mario, a male staff member was talking to a female staff member.

"'They think that he is going to get into rehab. What a joke,' he said.

"The man did not know that I was Mario's dad," Mark informed me.

"What did you do?" I asked.

"Nothing yet, I was too shocked to say anything," Mark replied.

Immediately after our talk, Mark went to the director's office and told her what had occurred. She said it would not happen again. Mark also told her that he did not want that man to work with Mario or visit him again. He stated that no one was to say anything negative in front of Mario, even if he was asleep. He told her that we were working against all the odds and were expecting a good recovery, no matter how long it took.

Mario's day went well. His grandparents had visited and wrote in the journal that he was alert and responsive. He did not have a fever and his heart rate was in the eighties.

However, that night the nurse called an ambulance to take Mario to the emergency room. Mario stayed all night at the hospital because he was not responsive to the nurse. At that time Mario was very limited on how he could respond to anything. He stayed all night in the hospital emergency room. He was returned to the nursing home in the morning. How terrifying for Mario! He had no way to communicate, didn't know what was going on, and was transported by strangers to an emergency room in an ambulance! We didn't even know what had happened until the next day.

It was no wonder that the entire day after the emergency room trip Mario was agitated. Our friends Kris and Richard Carson wrote in the journal that day:

"10:45 a.m. Mario seemed more agitated than usual. His heart rate was up and down. His temperature was 100.4. Richard read to him while I massaged his feet and legs. Hopefully he will feel more settled soon."

At 11:45 a.m. his grandparents came in and wrote: "Heart rate 140, eyes open, very agitated! Did R.O.M. on legs. Heart rate down to 110. He is now asleep, temperature 97.6."

1:00 p.m. Jenny wrote: "When I got here, Mark was here and he filled me in on the latest. The physical therapist Julie came in. She got Mario's arm way up into the air (straight) and she had him touch the top of his head and all over his face. When she went to the other arm, that is when he got agitated (heart rate 130). She got him to put his hands into the braces (2:30). When she left, Mario was really angry. He kept banging his left arm on the bed and kept trying to sit up.

"Tried to calm him down, but he seemed really frustrated. The nurses came in and moved Mario into a different position at around 2:45.

"When I came back at 3:00 p.m., Mario was a lot more relaxed. I sat down in the chair next to him and began to write in the book. He watched me for a little while and fell asleep. At 3:15 p.m. his heart rate is now at 95 bpm. I love you Mario. Jenny."

Later in the week Mark and I had our meeting with the nursing home staff about Mario. We met the speech pathologist and physical therapist. Mario would receive range of motion every day. He would also be put into a chair for at least an hour each day.

They gave us a videotape, "Living with a Tracheostomy," to view at home. We watched the one-hour tape for about ten minutes before turning it off. We decided that living with a trach tube was not something we were going to do. We agreed that Mario would get off the trach tube before he came home.

Trying Different Approaches to Stimulate Mario

There were so many new skills that we needed to learn. Since Mario was not able to get around by himself, we were the ones who had to move him. Getting Mario into a chair was no easy task. He had to be lifted up, using a machine called a Hoyer Lift. It uses hydraulics so you do not hurt your back moving a patient. Mario was dead weight and looked like a sack of potatoes. His muscle tone was gone and he had very little control of his body. Mario had also lost a lot of weight and was down to one hundred and twenty nine pounds. He was five feet ten inches, and beginning to look like someone from a concentration camp. He was always slim, but weighed one hundred and fifty five pounds at the time of the accident.

Seeing him in this helpless state broke my heart. What had happened to my handsome son? Would he ever return? Maybe a visit from his dog Freesia would help awaken Mario more.

Arrangements were made for Freesia to visit. She was twelve years old now and had slept in Mario's bed most of her life. He used to joke around, calling her his wife. She was a Basenji-Manchester terrier mix and extremely intelligent. We called her our gifted and talented dog.

When we brought Freesia into the nursing home she was very nervous. Mario was moved into a chair and we sat Freesia up on his lap. We got no response from Mario. He didn't even smile or try to pet her. This was a big disappointment. Did he not remember who she was? We will never know. Poor Freesia, she wagged her tail and licked Mario's face without a reaction. We took Freesia home feeling forlorn and depressed.

To encourage Mario to turn his head to the right we placed his bed by a window. In order to look out he had to turn his head. We also put family photos to the right side of his bed on the wall. I am not sure now that he could even see them. His vision was compromised and it took us about a year to figure out just how bad his vision was.

Today he wears glasses and they help some, but he still cannot track well enough to read a book. He has tunnel vision and uses only his left eye. If you tell Mario to look at something it takes him a long time to find the object, even if it is only a few feet away. He can type some, so he can send an e-mail, but someone has to read his e-mails back to him. His optometrist told me that as his brain heals, he has the possibility of having twenty/ twenty vision again.

In the two weeks that Mario stayed at the nursing home he was sent to the hospital emergency room three times! Mario got a bladder infection and his first bedsore while at the nursing home. He still has a scar on his right heel from that bed sore. Getting a bed sore is serious and can be life threatening because the infection can spread to other parts of the body.

One night when Mark went to visit, at about 6:00 p.m., Mario had not been given his evening medications. Mario needed a range of drugs to ease his pain and relax his body. It was important that he get his medications on time. He was starting to get agitated and his medications were past due. Mark asked the nurse to please give Mario his medications. She said she would. Another hour went by and it was now 8:00 p.m. Mario was beginning to sweat and his heart rate was elevated. Mark again found the night nurse and asked for Mario's medications. He told the nurse that Mario was in pain.

This time she got mad and said, "I will get there as soon as I can! I have one hundred and twenty patients to see and they are in pain too! You will just have to wait!"

Mario didn't get his medication until 10:30 p.m. He was one of the last patients to receive medications. We should have called our HMO and complained to the director, but we didn't. Now we wonder if receiving his medications late might have been the reason for the three trips back to the emergency room.

We need a Break

Mark and I were getting worn out. We had a lot of family and friends taking care of Mario and decided we needed to get away for the weekend. We chose a cute place in Monterey that some close friends had stayed at.

When I told my friend Virginia our plan she didn't think we should go and cautioned me: "Your love and energy are what is keeping Mario alive. I don't know what might happen if you go now."

I didn't want to listen and was desperate for a break so we went anyway. It was a mistake.

We took off work on Friday and drove down to Monterey. It is about a two-hour drive. I told my parents that we would call every night to get a report on Mario. They had our cell phone number if they needed to reach us.

It was warm for November and the sun was out. Mark and I got settled in our room and then went for a bike ride along the ocean. It was good for our souls and we felt like we had just been released from prison. After our bike ride we went to a kayak store. Besides horseback riding, one of our favorite things to do was kayak. We found a Kayak store and spent some time looking at the latest models and prices.

That night we checked in with my parents to see how it went with Mario. So far everything was "A okay." We went out to dinner and rented a movie. It was a romantic night. I felt rested and renewed, so I could give Mark the love and attention he so deserved.

On Saturday we bought tickets to the Monterey Bay Aquarium, a must see for anyone visiting the Monterey area. Using the fresh ocean water they are able to support an abundance of sea life with an amazing variety of sharks and fish. My favorite is the sunfish, which looks like a giant flat disk with the face of an alien. It measures about four feet in diameter.

We skipped lunch and went to El Torito for an early dinner. We were on vacation and it was a short walk back to our room. We thought that a pitcher of margaritas would go down well. As we sat sipping on our margaritas, looking out the window at the playful otters, life seemed good again.

Then the phone rang. It was my dad. Mario was back at the hospital and in ICU. My dad and Mario's aunt Irma had been there all day. Mario had been sent back to the hospital sometime in the early morning because of blood in his trach tube. When he arrived at the hospital his blood pressure and heart rate had gone sky high and they were having trouble getting them to go down, even with medication. I asked my dad if he thought we should come home. He suggested that we come home in the morning. There wasn't much we could do at the time and he would stay at the hospital until they got Mario stabilized.

I felt like I had been punched in the stomach. Couldn't we even take a brief respite? Mark and I finished the pitcher of margaritas and our meal, then we vowed to enjoy the time we had left and leave first thing in the morning. We would be home before noon.

It was another sleepless night. I couldn't stop thinking about Mario back in the ICU. What were we going to do? I prayed for an answer, never expecting what was to happen next.

Chapter 14

We Won't Take Him Back

I am happy to be alive. I want to teach the world the power of love and what you can accomplish with that power and that no one can copy or manipulate your love.

Mario

We got back to Mario's hospital at about 12:00 p.m. Mario was in stable condition, but still in the ICU. He would be moved back to a regular bed in a day or two. We went in to see him. He was all hooked up to life support machines and appeared to be sleeping. He was heavily sedated to keep his pulse and heart rate down. Now that he was stable they could slowly reduce the drugs.

I talked to Mario and told him we were back and how much we loved him. I prayed for him to recover quickly so he could return to the nursing home. We spent most of the day with Mario at the hospital. It was Sunday and there was no point in going to the nursing home until Monday to find out why they had sent him back to the hospital in the first place.

I took the day off work and my dad went with me to talk to the director of the home. She told us how sorry she was about what had occurred. Apparently the night nurse found blood in his trach tube, so she called 911. By the time he got to the hospital his pulse and heart rate were out of control. She also informed us that they could not take Mario back. Her staff felt that his problems were too severe for them to take care of him properly. It would be best for everyone if we found another placement.

I knew there was not another place that our HMO would pay for, so I begged for another try. "Please take Mario back. He is comfortable here and we just got his room set up. We cannot take him home in this condition. It will only be for a few months, just until we get him into a rehabilitation facility."

Her response was, "I am sorry but we cannot do that, it is not in your son's best interest."

At the time I was angry and confused. What were we going to do with Mario? Little did I know what a blessing it was. Going back to the hospital would eventually get him to a rehabilitation facility, but it would be another five weeks before this would happen.

On Tuesday Mario was moved to the third floor of our hospital into a regular bed. I called Gina and Nicole and they helped us move all his things back from the nursing home. At the home the staff asked if we wanted to take the medical supplies and liquid canned food.

"Why would I want to do that"? I questioned.

"Because it will just be thrown out," said the nurse.

Because of some law, they cannot reuse the food or supplies even when unopened. What a waste! I wonder just how much perfectly good stuff gets dumped every day. We loaded up bags of supplies and about four cases of food.

Now I had to call all the family and friends to let them know where Mario was. It was important to get his visitors back on schedule so we could continue his therapy. Who knew how long he would remain at the hospital?

The hospital discharge nurse was looking for another placement for Mario. At least he had a private room now because of the staph infection that he carried on his body.

The hospital nurses now wanted all of us to wear hospital gowns, masks and gloves when we visited. How annoying! We complied with wearing the gowns and gloves, but took the masks off as soon as no one was watching. A special bed that changed Mario's body position every fifteen minutes followed him from the nursing home to the hospital. It looked much more comfortable and we hoped it would prevent him from getting more bedsores.

It was good to be back on the third floor where some of the nurses had been so kind to Mario. Nurse Solon was happy to have Mario back and determined to get him into rehab.

We had to get him to respond to a doctor. This would be our main goal.

"Mario, raise your arm if you want music. Mario, raise your arm if you have pain," I would coach him.

Sometimes he would respond, but not consistently.

CHAPTER 15

Conversations with a Nurse

Be the answer to someone else's prayer.

Quote from the Divine Source

I talked with Nurse Solon and below is what he had to say about Mario's stay at the hospital:

Mario was different. We didn't get any patients in the condition of Mario. He was very young and most of our patients were elderly and dying or had other severe complications they were recovering from in the ICU unit. Mario was completely different. The moment I saw Mario there was something unique about him. Maybe it was because he was young and I enjoy kids. It was a change from taking care of people who were dying. It was an extreme challenge taking care of Mario. Nobody wanted to work with Mario. He had a trach and had just experienced a catastrophic accident and intensive care. He had so many medications and they all had to be put through a feeding tube. Mario was not the most cooperative person. There were a lot of visitors all day long and nobody knew how to deal them. This was something new to the floor. No one was used to so many people coming in to administer healing and massages."

In the hospital the news was that Mario was a vegetable. He was there until they could find a place to farm him out. The goal was to get him a little better so they could transfer him to a board and care facility. There was not much emphasis put on Mario as a person. He wasn't getting physical therapy or any extras. Opinions on Mario's prognosis were about fifty-fifty. Some doctors wanted to try to help and some basically thought it was a lost cause. I had to talk to one doctor and tell him it was inappropriate to refer to Mario as a vegetable in front of him. He apologized to me and said I was right. I told him that nobody really knew if Mario was able to understand or not.

I would check in on Mario at least five times a week, even if I was working. I wanted to make sure he had his music, because I like music too. I wanted to make sure he was comfortable. Often I would find him on the bed, half naked with his sheet at his feet. I would cover him, talked to him and made sure he was comfortable.

For some reason, when I came into the room he was a lot more quiet and cooperative than he was with other people. There was always a connection between us. I thought it was really great. He was a really big challenge for me. He was a reaffirmation to me about what I should do with my life.

I was a nursing student at the time and not sure I had made the right decision. It was a difficult time in my life. I was studying, working and being a single parent raising my daughter. Mario was validation that I had made the right decision; in fact I became a pediatric nurse.

It was a great time to meet Mario. He was there for a reason for me. I had come out of a comma once and knew what it was like to not be able to move my body and communicate. Your nerve endings are not able to control that part of your body so you cannot talk. You can think things but have no control over your body. It is really frustrating and I knew Mario understood me. He was just a pissed off kid.

The moment I realized that Mario did understand me, I knew he could be helped. I knew something could be done for Mario. It just depended on how much his family was going to push for it and how hard Mario would work for it. I knew because he listened to me. He helped me by cooperating when I had to change his sheets, brush his teeth or bathe him. He did not have the tantrums like he did with other people.

As time went on, we got him to answer with yes and no. He raised his left arm for yes and shook his head for no. From that time on it was a lot easier to deal with him. He still would not cooperate with a lot of people and the doctors didn't believe he understood because they had not seen it.

Mario would get pissed off when the doctors came into the room and would just lay there with no affect. I talked to him about how important it was to respond to the doctors. I told him he wasn't going to get anywhere unless he cooperated. We used to have really long talks. I knew that he could respond, but when it came to "show and tell" for the doctors, he wouldn't do anything.

This experience has changed my life. It has made me a better person. It made me become a nurse. Having Mario in my life is one of the greatest things I will ever have. He was meant to be there for me.

He has changed a lot of people's lives. There is a lot of love and it is great. Basically that is what my job is about, one person at a time. You change one persons' life and it means the world.

Modeling headshot of Mario, 2001.

Mario's sexy dude look.
Modeling photo taken in 2001.

Modeling picture of Mario the all American guy, 2001.

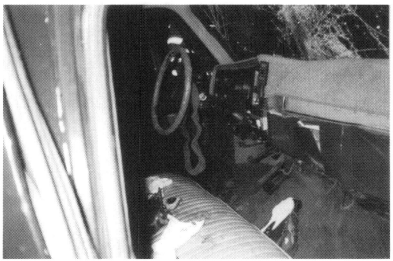

Mario's crashed truck, August 8, 2002.

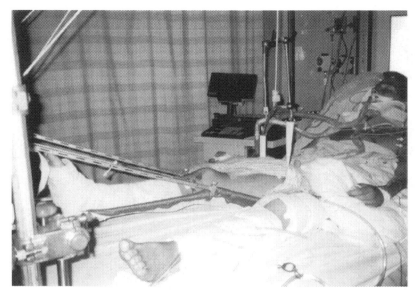

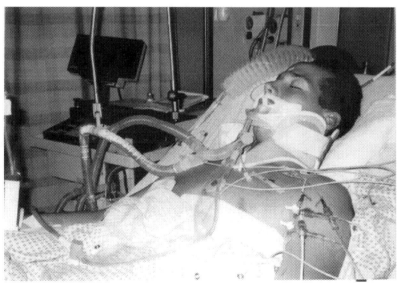

Mario in ICU, August 2002.

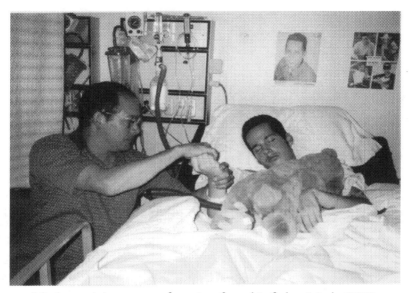

Mario receiving range of motion from his father Mark, 2002.

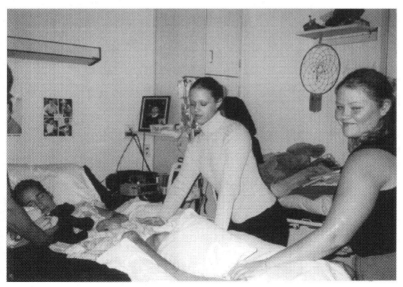

Gina and Nicole with Mario in the hospital, 2002.

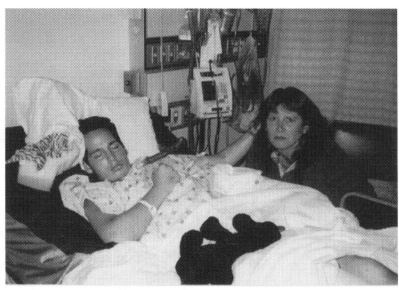

Mario puts his hand on his mother Christine for the first time, 2002.

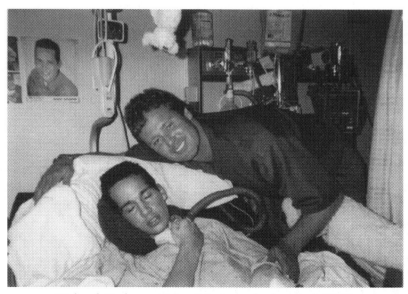

Richard Carlson visiting Mario in the hospital, 2002.

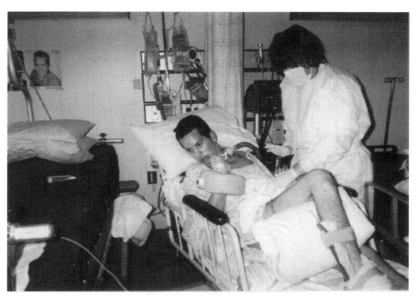

Mario the pretzel boy at the nursing home, October 2002.

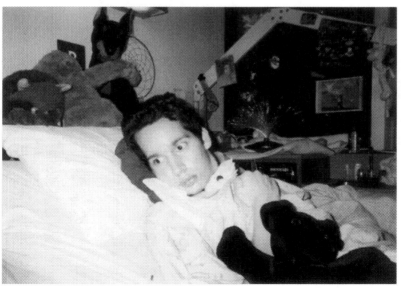

Mario at rehab, December 2002.

Mario with his dog Freesia visiting him at rehab, December 2002.

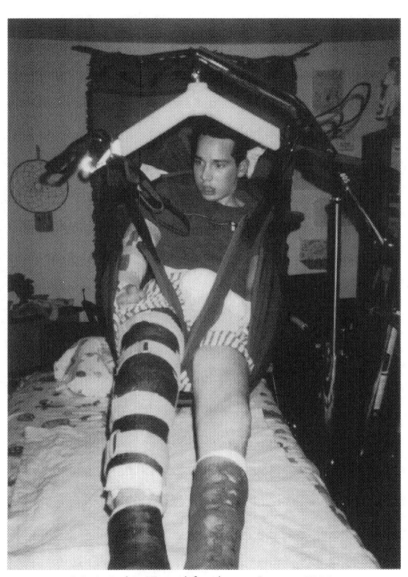

Mario in his Hoyer lift at home, January 2003.

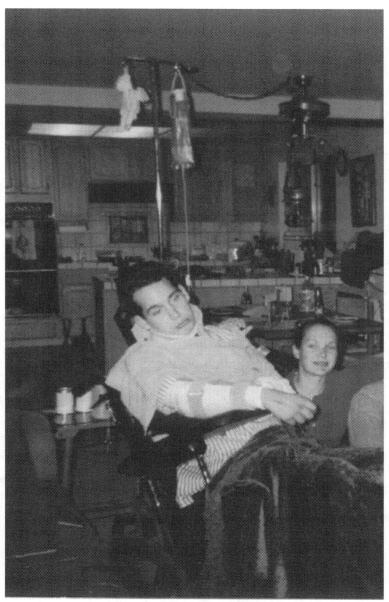

Mario at home with Stephanie, January 2003

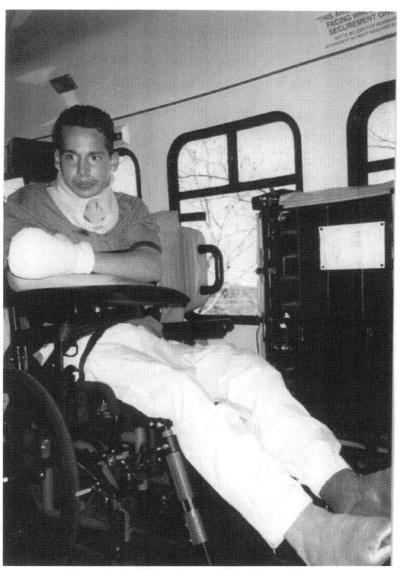

Mario on the bus to rehab, February 2003.

Mario in his tilt wheel chair with Ana and Sola, February 2003.

Mario with the Carlson family, Kris, Jasmine, and Richard, April 2003.

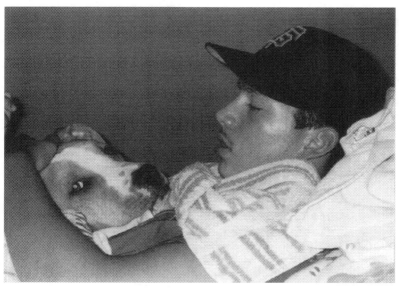

Mario with his dog Sola in bed, 2003.

Mario petting his dog Sola, 2003.

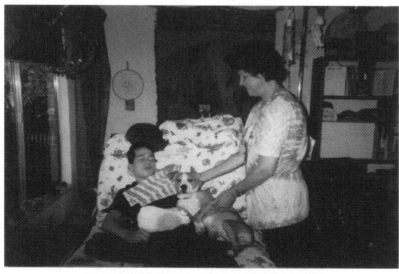

Our friend Michelle visiting Mario, 2003.

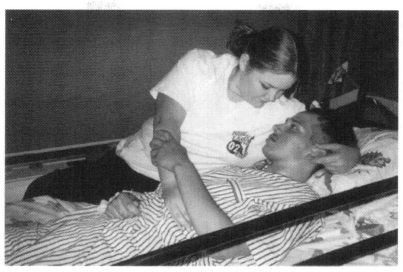

Mario's friend Nicole visiting
Mario at home, 2003.

Mario playing tug of war with his new puppy Sola, 2003

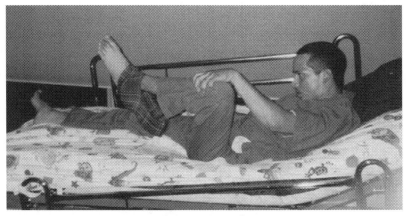

Mario doing range of motion
using a beanbag, 2003.

Daddy Mark and Ana bathing Mario outside, April 2003.

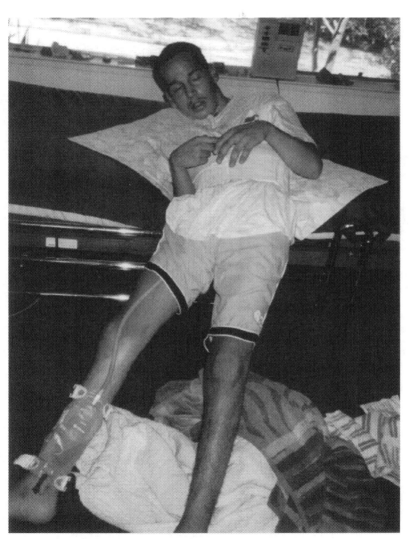

Stiff as a board and exhausted after raging, 2003.

Mario in a beach wheel chair with Sola pulling him, 2004.

Mario at the Devil's Golf Course in Death Valley, December 2005.

Mario on Sunshine with his mother and care giver, 2005.

Old time photo at Calico, December 2005.

Christmas parade at Death
Valley, December 2005.

Mario and Sola with grandmother Helen Scharmer, 2008.

Mario rock climbing, 2008.

Mario out to lunch with grandma Bette, grandpa Jim and mother, 2007.

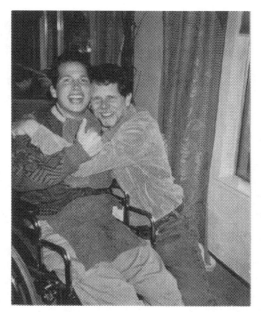

Mario with his uncle Marc, December 2007.

Mario bike riding in Yosemite with his brother Miguel, 2009.

Mario on his new bike at Solano Lake, 2009.

Mario swimming at the Y.M.C.A. with his buddies Eric and Mike, 2009.

CHAPTER 16

Too Late For Shoes

"Hope in your hands, that's how you live"... with tears in your eyes but you still give... You give cause its good... It fills the space in your heart like food for the soul... You give with no expectations... No rewards... And no demands... This is how I want to be... Show me how to see... teach me how to love... I look to you behind the layers of my cornea but you will never know it... U need not to find me because I am always close... U almost lost one but through strength you rose and have overcome many obstacles in this lifetime... When tested you can start off as one of the weakest players and end one of the strongest... You may never know but everything I have good in me and give to others has come from you... "Hope in your hands that's how you live..."

Miguel Scharmer

We continued our personalized physical therapy schedule for Mario with about five visitors a day. Everyone was writing in the journal about how much more responsive Mario was. He was tracking with his eyes, making more body movements, and responding to questions.

When someone read to him a list of tunes, he could raise his arm if he wanted to listen to one. There would be setbacks now and then with fever, sweats, and high heart rate, but for the most part he kept moving forward.

When he would regress it would usually happen after a move. Three times in one week we walked into Mario's room only to find someone else in his bed, or an empty room! This was totally unnecessary and scared me to death. Each time I would freak out thinking Mario was back in the ICU or perhaps dead. There didn't seem to be a good reason to move him so much. I complained to our favorite doctor. The one who had been the most helpful when Mario was first injured. He said he would put it in his chart to not move Mario any more. Thank God it worked.

We also requested that Mario get braces or splints for his right arm and leg and Botox injections to reduce his tone. Tone is extreme tightness in the limbs of the body, which is caused by the brain injury.

My brother had sent me treatment information on traumatic brain injury (TBI) that he had found on the Internet.

Those articles recommended the use of Botox to reduce tone in tight muscles of brain-injured patients. Our doctor asked the powers that be, but both requests were denied.

This kind doctor knew we were trying to get Mario to a rehabilitation facility and said he would help, but Mario had to be able to follow simple commands for a doctor referral. The same doctor made arrangements to have Mario sit in a chair each day after our request.

At first, sitting was difficult for Mario, but after one week he could tolerate one hour at a time! He also got the respiratory therapist to plug Mario's trach tube so he could practice breathing on his own. Again this was at our request.

When the trach tube was plugged, we encouraged Mario to speak, but no sound emerged. Every day Mario's trach tube was plugged a little longer. Someone had to sit with Mario during this time.

The hospital staff did not have time, so we made sure it was done every day we were there to visit. If Mario had trouble with secretions we would call for help immediately. We went from a few minutes, up to an hour. If we hadn't asked for the extras and been willing to sit with him and help, these treatments would not have been administered. Mario did not talk, but by plugging his trach tube we moved that much closer to getting it removed.

I went to a class on the brain one weekend and met a wonderful woman whose son Michael had sustained a traumatic brain injury (TBI). He had fallen one hundred feet from a rock onto his head. It was a miracle that he survived. After only a year of rehabilitation he was walking, talking and going to school. He suffered from memory loss and lived with his mother because he could not drive or organize his life.

Both the woman and her son came to visit Mario.

This is what Michael had to say: "I want to be there for you... Please use me as a source of strength for you. I will be there for you and your family. Just call me any time."

They were there for us and even brought Mario high top tennis shoes. Michael's mom told us that if you do not take care of the feet right from the start, foot drop occurs after a period of time. Foot drop is the inability to raise the front part of the foot due to weakness, lack of use or paralysis of the muscles that lift the foot. The ankle and toes turn downward. We didn't know just how important it was to take care of Mario's feet. The hospital hadn't done their job.

Most hospitals are set up for short-term treatment. Nursing homes are for warehousing long-term patients, so Mario's feet were neglected. This was why nurse Solon had insisted that we get Mario to a rehabilitation facility.

The shoes were a wonderful gesture of love, but it was **too late for shoes**. When Mario finally got to rehab, he would have to have surgery to correct his foot problems. This could have been prevented with early intervention.

I mentioned that Mario was moved often and without our notification. One of the moves was to a hospital bed next to the nursing station. This should be good we thought. The head nurse told us that they could keep a closer eye on Mario and would even have the pulse oximeter facing the door so they could easily read it.

While in this room, several of Mario's visitors wrote that when they came in to see Mario, the machine was turned off! We were paying for this machine out of pocket and the staff didn't even bother to turn it on. Was communication that poor between shifts or did the staff just not care?

In this room Mario had a roommate, a retired army general who was dying of lung cancer. He had been a heavy smoker and according to his kids never was pleasant to be around. He was very demanding. He made a lot of noise and all of Mario's visitors found the fellow annoying. This is what Mario's friend Gina had to say about the man next door:

"Mario is sleeping, for the first time in a long time. It's just him and I. His heart rate is at 74 bpm, so he is really relaxed at the moment. Some healers are supposed to come today, but I have yet to see them. Oh yeah, and Mario has shoes on today. And the guy next to us is really loud! Will someone shoot him with a dart? All he does is cough and cough. I'm surprised Mario doesn't wake up and throw his shoe at him. I know that's what I would be doing right about now, but then again, I'm mean. Anyway, back to Mario. I can't wait until you're all better. I miss you a lot even though you thought Nikki was an angel and I was the demon spawn. At the time that we were together my mind was on you, but I got scared that you were like all the rest. Now I'm trying not to be selfish. I don't know if it's working. Anyway, I can't wait till your better, where you can walk and talk and be how you were. Even if you do still hate me. You get better all the time. Keep up the good work."

Both Gina and Niki continued to support Mario for years to follow. They came on a regular basis, both to the rehabilitation facility and later to our home. They are both angels in my book.

Mark and I have found that you have to push, push, push and advocate when working with hospitals or HMOs. If you don't, your loved one could be lost in the shuffle. It is a sad thing to think of how many lives are wasted because no one is willing to put in the time or money to help.

To this day Mark and I always have to research and come up with new ideas and therapies for Mario. He keeps slowly improving and his needs keep changing. We have to ask for everything. If we stop asking nothing new happens. It is not easy. I had to retire early at fifty-five to keep up with the demands. Not everyone has that luxury.

Something we didn't try, but heard about later, was to put a box of candy in the patient's room with a nice note. The note might read, "Dear nurses, thank you for all your hard work." Whenever someone comes into the room for a piece of candy, they are more likely to check on the patient.

Anything that you can do to advocate for your loved one is important. Hospital and nursing staffs are often over-worked. Everyone wants to be appreciated, and as my father says, "You can catch more flies with honey than vinegar."

Chapter 17

Rehab

Tangled up in everyday decisions... Why do I have to learn the hard way... Life is full of tests? Do we pass them, as we should? Who are we to judge? Thirty percent of our life we sleep... another thirty percent we work... ten percent we eat... another ten percent we handle business... and the last twenty percent we get to enjoy to ourselves. Where does the time go... Never take any moment for granted for every day may be our last. Take the time to tell your loved ones how you really feel about them. Time is not something all of us have...

Miguel Scharmer

After one hundred and forty-one days, we were finally moving Mario to a rehabilitation facility! We were all grateful that it was happening and hopeful that Mario would now get the care he so desperately needed.

The rehab facility was only forty-five minutes from our home, an easy commute. Arrangements were made for Mario's transport and this time the move went smoothly. We said our goodbyes to many of the hospital staff and gave Solon hugs and kisses. I rode in the ambulance with Mario, while Gina, Nicole and Miguel helped Mark with all of Mario's stuff.

When we got to the facility we met with an intake doctor and he evaluated Mario. He seemed concerned that Mario was not able to do more, and wanted to know our expectations. He kept asking us what our long-range plans were for Mario and where he was going to go after rehab.

"You are taking him home after here, aren't you?" The doctor asked.

"No," I replied, "He cannot come home until he can walk and take care of himself. We both work full time and cannot take care of Mario. Maybe he can go back to a nursing home for a while."

"If you send him back to a nursing home you will loose everything that you gained here at rehab," cautioned the doctor." "He needs to go home after rehab."

We told the doctor that we would think about taking him home. He said they would train us and have the social worker contact us about in-home support services. We were given a list of supplies to bring for Mario right away: slippers, shirts, sweatpants, underwear, toothbrush, brush, shampoo, soap, deodorant, etc. We were told that Mario would be put on a regular schedule for classes and bathing. He would not be disturbed at night, like in a hospital, and would even get to sleep with the lights out. I had heard from a former rehab patient that just getting good sleep often created miracles.

We went home that night with our heads spinning about what to do with Mario after rehab. The estimated time of his stay was from forty to sixty days as an inpatient. He could return as an outpatient as long as he continued to improve and reach the goals that were set for him. But bring him home, how could we?

I worked full time as a schoolteacher and our life style had been designed for a two-income household. Besides our house payment, we had two horses to provide for. Our medical insurance alone was $1000 a month. We did have some savings, and for short term, I could take sick leave days. Mark's business was always slow in the winter, so he could help more with Mario initially. I did get a summer vacation, so maybe it was a possibility.

In our minds, Mario was going to have a full recovery in one or two years. With this goal in place, we started thinking about bringing Mario home.

Most rehab facilities are set up to provide intensive inpatient therapy from one to six months. Rarely are patients kept longer. It is very expensive, and long-term therapy requires family intervention. Mario was fortunate to have a family to support him.

We returned to rehab the next morning and got to see Mario get his first shower in four months! He was carefully moved into a tilt shower chair. Mario was very unsure about the move and his eyes got as big as saucers. Plastic had to be taped over his feeding tube to protect it from getting wet.

Very quickly and efficiently the nurse's aide scrubbed Mario head to toe. I sang "Down at the Car Wash," substituting Mario for car. Humor always lightened every experience and Mark and I were becoming experts at comic relief. Mario started to relax more and more as the warm water poured over his body.

Mario had always been a very clean-cut teenager and would often take two showers a day. Mark and I used to get annoyed at the "waste" of water. How many times had we "sweated the small stuff" in our lives? After his shower, he was dressed and then off to occupational therapy, his first class.

The occupational therapist placed many different objects in front of Mario. He asked Mario to grab one. There was a ball, toy car, brush, glass, etc. Mario looked at the objects but would not respond when asked to pick one up.

The occupational therapist asked us what Mario might like to have? We suggested money. He then told Mario that if he could pick up the dollar on the table it was his. After several attempts he reached out and picked up the money. We were all clapping and cheering. Leave it to Mario to go for the money. I saved the dollar, taping it into one of the journals, which we kept in his room. The same day after taking the dollar, Mario was able to grab a glass too!

Christmas was in three days, so we decided to decorate his room with presents and a tree. I had brought home a little artificial tree from school. We put up decorations that my students had made for Mario, along with some low heat lights. Someone had given Mario a "porcupine atmosphere" night-light that was really cool to look at. All his cards and toys were also put on a table by the tree in his room. The room was full of love and hope. Mark took Mario's stuffed bear and wrapped its arms around a life-size stuffed dog that looked like Freesia. There wasn't another patient's room at this facility with as much love energy as Mario's. We also brought some of his favorite tunes and my relaxation CDs to be played for him.

Christmas Day, there were no classes, so we decided to bring Freesia and take Mario outside on a walk. We bundled him up and covered him with a blanket. He wore a yellow sweatshirt and a black beanie on his head. He had not been outside in four months. He seemed to enjoy being outside. He had a special tilt wheelchair, so he was pretty comfortable.

Mario had his trach tube plugged, which was the first thing rehab did when he arrived.

The doctor even commented about it. "Why does he still have a trach tube? He wasn't having any problems breathing."

"That's what we had asked," I replied.

The plan was to take the trach tube out in four or five days.

Mario was not able to hold up his head and he drooled a lot. His tongue was flaccid and would have to be trained if he was ever going to eat by mouth again. Mark and I put a headband on Mario and tied it to the back of his headrest on the wheelchair to keep his head up.

Mario's brain kept contracting his body forward, causing a lot of tone (muscle tightness). His right hand and arm were still clenched and his right leg was bent. He had foot drop in both feet. All of these issues would have to be addressed if Mario was ever going to recover and walk again.

We thought it might be interesting to see if Mario responded differently to seeing his dog. We were delighted to see that this time when Mario saw Freesia he responded! We set the dog in the back of the Jeep and moved his chair close so he could reach her. He grabbed her paw and petted her for ten minutes. We told Mario we were going to get him a new dog, something small, maybe a poodle that he could sleep with when he came home. Yes home. We had decided that Mario would be coming home.

After Christmas Mario started his rehab classes again. He was put on a tilt board so he could get used to being in a standing position. This went well. At occupational therapy, he picked up a spoon, fork, and flashlight on command. During his speech time the teacher put a cold popsicle stick in his mouth to try to get his tongue to move. He was furious and bit the stick, shook his head, and growled like a dog. At least we got some sound out of him.

The social worker at the rehab center met with us to see if she could get Mario enrolled in MediCal and SSI. Under MediCal he would receive in-home support service hours, so we could hire workers at $8.50 an hour to help with his care. We were fortunate to have a social worker to help navigate us through this bureaucracy.

On December 31st, Mario was scheduled for an MRI. We were happy to be getting more information about his brain damage. Unfortunately, he freaked out and they were not able to get an image.

The Wonderful Dr. K

Mario's rehab doctor was new to California and our HMO. She was a New Yorker and told us right from the start that as long as Mario kept making progress she would see to it that he received services. She kept her word and even after seven years Mario goes back as an outpatient for therapy when we ask for it. When we feel he needs new exercises or goals, I call her up, make an appointment, and she gets us right in.

Back at the hospital we had asked for Botox, splints, and other drugs to help with his contractions. This doctor gave Mario all of the above. She remembers how Mario came in and refers to him as the "pretzel boy." Mario is her "miracle patient." She says that she always has a great day after seeing Mario.

One day, while Mario was at the center, she told us she had a dream that Mario spoke to her. How many doctors dream about their patients and share the dream with the family? We owe this doctor a lot and will always be grateful to her.

Dr. K, as I will call her, knew that Mark and I were exhausted and encouraged us to take a vacation while he was at rehab. I told the doctor about the experience we had the last time we took a needed break, how Mario almost died while he was at the nursing home.

She said he would have much better care at the rehab center than in a nursing home. She explained that once we got him home it would be harder to get away.

"Go some place close to home and check on him every day by phoning," she suggested.

Mark and I decided to go to Inn of the Tides at Bodega Bay for two nights. It was only an hour from the rehab center and one and a half hours from our house.

Before we left, Mario had his trach tube removed permanently! I thought that it was a good sign that this vacation would be better.

Chapter 18

Release Me

There is a lot of me inside of you. Open the lids your eyes hide behind and see... You were meant for me and now I can finally see...No sense of reason, no knowledge of shame.. Your silence haunts me at night and makes it hard to get a wink of sleep...Your smiles take me away to a far off place I've never been before.. Is this all an optical illusion??? I hope not... The eyes show us what the brain wants us to see... But when matters turn to the heart all thoughts must surrender to love... For if it is love let it strike true and hard...

Miguel Scharmer

The trip to Bodega Bay was just what we needed. It was our time to nest and snuggle. We slept in each morning and awoke to a gorgeous view of the ocean and bay. Walks on the beach, with all of the sounds of the ocean, have a way of deeply nurturing our psyches and healing emotional wounds.

The weather had remained clear for us and so far every phone call to check in on Mario had confirmed no problems. We spent two delightful nights at the Inn of the Tides. January 3rd, on our anniversary, we returned home.

It was our seventeenth wedding anniversary. Mark was a second marriage for me. He had come free of baggage, with a three-bedroom house and pool! I brought two boys and the complications of an ex-husband.

Mark never faltered from the task of raising the boys. He had stepped up and even adopted them when their birth father gave permission. Now our marriage was being tested to the limit. Could it stand an assault like this? I prayed Mark would stand by me and not run like so many people do in a crisis situation.

Back at Rehab, Again

On the way home, we decided to stop at the rehab facility and meet with Dr. K. She had planned on giving Mario his first set of Botox injections in his arm and hand before casting them. Mario's muscle tone was so severe that his right hand stayed clenched in a fist most of the time. His arm was also clamped against his chest.

One friend of mine had commented that it was almost like Mario was still hanging on to the steering wheel of his truck, preparing for a crash. If he was ever going to get any use of that arm, it had to be released.

It was not easy giving Mario the shots. Dr. K had Mark and I stay to assist. She explained to Mario what she was going to do and why. Mark held his left hand to keep it down. The doctor pulled his locked arm out as far as she could and muscle tested him with an electric meter to try and find the best injection site.

The needle was the longest one we had ever seen. It was frightening to look at. When the doctor inserted the needle Mario had a look of extreme discomfort. His mouth gapped open and his eyes sent a message of shear pain. I cried as I watched. How much more would my baby boy have to endure? It hurt him so much, but the poor thing couldn't even scream. No sound came from him. This whole episode took only about five minutes, but it seemed endless.

Advice for Rough Times

For me as a mother, my most difficult times have been seeing my children suffer. As a mother I want my children to have a happy, pain-free life. This is a shear impossibility for anyone living in a body.

So what can you do during the rough times? Give your children unlimited, unconditional love. Assure them that they are never alone. Teach them that they have control over their lives by the choices they make, the friends they associate with, and the attitudes they keep.

Help them learn to follow their heart, keep hope alive, help each other, forgive, and love. This is the best advice you can offer anyone.

After the injections we got Mario comfortable by talking to him and playing a little music. After about thirty minutes we took him outside on a walk. I picked a flower for Mario and gave it to him to smell. He seemed to enjoy it and held onto it for about ten minutes or so before he dropped it.

Mario always had to have a towel draped around his shoulders to catch the drool that would run down his mouth and neck.

It was on this day that Mark got a terrific idea. "Let's see if we can get Mario to hold onto the towel while we pull him. This will give him some control over his body and surroundings. It might even be fun for Mario," he said.

We put the towel in Mario's left hand and told him to hold on while we pulled. He held on! At first the towel would slip out, but we would gently replace it and away we would go.

Mario got better and better at this game and soon we were cruising all over the rehab grounds with Mario in tow. I would guide the back of the chair and Mark would pull. He really seemed to enjoy this and it would become a regular, fun way to travel when we would visit.

Later we got Mario a handle to hold on to. It was actually a rubber tug toy that I had purchased for our new puppy. Yes puppy. She was home waiting for us. She was not the small little lap dog I had envisioned.

CHAPTER 19

Pound Puppy

Smile because somebody loves you.

Mario

We had a new puppy now. When it was time to start looking for a dog, being the spiritual person that I am, I had to visualize, meditate, and affirm my intentions on what kind of dog I wanted. My mind was focused on a small shorthaired female, not more than fifteen or twenty pounds. What I asked for was a therapy dog to help with the healing of Mario.

"Please send us an angel dog. Let me know without a doubt when we have found the right dog," I prayed.

Big Dogs, No Thanks!

We had seen many therapy dogs at the rehab center. Some were in training. Most of them were Labradors or some sort of Labrador mix. These dogs were very expensive. Mark and I were not prepared to buy one.

We knew we didn't want a large dog. I have never liked large breed dogs. I always felt a little intimidated by them.

Why didn't I want a large breed dog? This story goes back to when I was sixteen visiting my uncle on a ranch in Wyoming. The ranch dog, a beautiful German shepherd, had attacked me. The dog had been friendly in the morning, but for some reason when we returned from dinner in town, it jumped up at my throat when I walked toward the front door. My uncle had responded quickly and hit the dog with a bucket so it backed off. After that experience I felt very threatened by big dogs, especially Shepherds.

Our last two dogs, Freesia and Mochi, had both been adopted as adults. Freesia was a Basenji/Manchester Terrier mix and Mochi was a little black Pug mix. We loved our dogs dearly and really preferred to rescue a dog rather than purchase a purebred puppy.

We wanted a shorthaired dog for the low maintenance. Living on four acres of grass with an endless supply of foxtails can be a real hazard for any dog. Even with our two little shorthaired mutts, we had experienced foxtails in the eyes, ears, and anus, ouch!

Every Saturday we began the search for the perfect dog for Mario. We started at the local pet stores where rescued dogs were on display. Most of the dogs were big and some type of pit bull mix, yuck! We took Freesia with us so we could make sure the new dog would get along with her too. No dogs were found that would work for our situation.

One day after visiting three different stores our son Miguel said, "Why don't we look at the pound?"

" No, I don't want to go there." I replied.

"Why not? You could save a life," said Miguel.

"I can't stand to see the animals in cages," I said.

Miguel commented, "Let's just go and look." So off to the pound we went.

It was January and the building was very cold. Most of the caged animals were shivering. It had been so cold that there had been television newscasts asking people to donate old blankets or towels to help keep the dogs warm.

Mark and Miguel walked around and surveyed the scene. I was very reluctant to even look into the cages. My heart was open, but my eyes did not want to see. Slowly I walked over to one cage that had about four young dogs in it. There were three Shepherd mixes and one golden girl sitting way in the back. Her eyes met mine and I knew she was the one. My heart melted and I felt a warm unconditional love pour over my body like liquid honey. Tears of joy came to my eyes. I couldn't hold back the flood of tears. I was so overwhelmed with love. This was our therapy dog!

I coaxed the dog over to the door of the cage. The other dogs were trying to get my attention, but I only had eyes for her. It was a female and she was beautiful. She had a fawn color to her coat with a white stripe down her face, four white socks and a white snip at the end of her tail. Time stopped as we sat and stared into each other's eyes.

Mark and Miguel came over. "Mark, this is the dog," I said, through tears of joy.

" What, how do you know?" He questioned.

"I just know. Trust me," I replied.

By now my husband was used to my wacky ways and said, "Okay, I'll go find someone to help us."

It turned out that the dog had just been picked up the day before in Antioch, a city about fifteen miles away. The policy was to hold each dog for one week in case someone claimed him/ her. The staff veterinarian guessed that the dog was about three months old and a Pit Bull/Lab mix. She would not be ready for adoption for another week. It would be first come, first serve.

Mark asked me if I was sure I wanted a Pit mix.

I said, " I know it sounds crazy, but I don't care what she is, that is the right dog for Mario."

We filled out some paperwork declaring our interest in the dog. We could come and visit her every day if we wished. The poor dog had to stay caged up in the cold for an entire week while we waited. I felt pretty sure no one would claim her, but it was still hard to wait a week.

School was back in session so Mark did most of the visiting since I was teaching all day. His business is slow in the winter.

Every time Mark went to visit she got a little friendlier.

One night when Mark came home he said, "That puppy is a real nice dog."

He even took his secretary to meet her and she fell in love too. "Chris, you have got to get that dog," she said.

Adoption day came and Mark got up at 5:00 a.m. to be the first one at the pound. The doors opened at 7:00 a.m. and thank God no one else wanted our little pit puppy. Papers were signed and fees paid, but we would still have to wait another three days for her surgery.

When you adopt any animal from the pound it must be spayed or neutered before you can have it. When we finally got the little girl she was drugged and recovering from her surgery.

"I sure hope you made the right decision," my doubting mind whispered.

After the puppy's surgery we brought her home and put her in a little bed next to our old dog Freesia. Freesia was very kind to the little girl, who at three months already weighed twenty-five pounds.

She had huge feet and everyone that met her kept saying that she was going to be a big dog. I refused to believe that and responded by saying she wasn't going to be bigger than forty-five pounds, ha ha! Today Sola weighs in at eighty pounds!

The First Sola

How did we pick the name Sola? When Mario was sixteen he got a job selling newspapers. He mostly worked on the weekends and sometimes after school. On one cold rainy day he was selling newspaper subscriptions in Antioch at a shopping center. A young dog kept coming into the building and the storekeeper wanted to call the pound. Mario tied the dog up so it wouldn't leave and made friends with it. He asked the store manager not to call the pound. He would take the dog home. The only problem was, Mario had not asked us.

We got a phone call. "Mom I have found a lost dog. She is cold and I want to bring her home," Mario stated.

"No!" I said. "We already have two dogs. There is no place to keep her. Our yard isn't even fenced to keep a large dog in."

"Please mom, just until we find her a home, Mario pleaded."

"Mario do not bring the dog home," I demanded. Well Mario never did listen to reason, so of course he brought the dog home.

She was a beautiful German shorthaired hunting dog. Mario had named her Sola because she was all alone ("sola" means alone in Spanish).

Mario begged us to keep the dog. We said "No, no, no!" But not wanting the dog to go to the pound, I called the local newspaper and posted an add. I prayed that the owners would be contacted soon so we could get rid of the dog.

Sola number one was very smart and began to follow us around the yard wherever we went. My husband was impressed at her ability to learn. She did not hurt our chickens, but would point when she saw them. After a week with Sola we were beginning to give in to Mario and were considering adopting her. Mario said he would pay all the veterinarian bills for her shots and getting spayed.

One week later, the phone rang. It was the owner. She had seen the advertisement in the newspaper. We made arrangements for her to pick up the dog on Saturday.

When she and her husband came to get the dog we were surprised that Sola didn't run to greet them! I felt no heart connection with them and was concerned about Sola's lack of interest. Sola stayed curled up by the fireplace in her comfortable bed and stared at us. Finally after several attempts of calling her she reluctantly went over to them.

Who were these people? How could we let Sola go with them, I pondered?

The owner's husband put Sola on a leash, thanked us and walked out the door.

As they were leaving the man said. "Next time we chain that dog up like I told you so she can't get out again."

I had tears in my eyes. My husband and I vowed that if we ever found a dog again without tags, that we liked, we would keep it and not look for the owner. It was a good thing Mario was not at home when the dog was picked up. He would have been furious.

When we found our therapy dog there was no question that her name should be Sola. This was Mario's dog and she too, like the first Sola, had been found alone in the City of Antioch on a cold rainy day.

It was January 25th when we took Sola to visit Mario at rehab. Mario had been spitting and drooling a lot, so Sola, being a puppy, cleaned him right up. Mario loved the attention from his new dog. He was able to scratch her nose and grab her ear and leg, pulling it in a petting motion. Sola just wagged her tail.

Some of the nurses at the hospital were very worried about us getting a puppy for Mario.

"Be careful that the puppy doesn't chew Mario's toes or casts off! He cannot move, and puppies like to chew," one nurse said.

Oh my God, I would never have thought of that! We had just a few more days and Mario would be coming home. Was getting a puppy a mistake? Time would tell.

CHAPTER 20

Coming Home

Half way up... Or half way down... Which half are
you...?
Shall I fake it half way just to fit into your world... Or
do I dare to be the man I do not fully understand, but
strain to be...
I want to make a difference in this crazy world we
call home... Let the angels cry out their tunes of
prosperous harmony as I vast down the valley of the
prosperous...
I am no longer bound by your words... Chained with
your thoughts... Or stuck with your thoughts... I am
free for all I believe is the Karma that comes back to
me...
Strip me down to my bare soul, but you can never
take the inner side of me...

Miguel Scharmer

Before we could bring Mario home there were lots of preparations to
make. We needed ramps to get him in and out of the house and a room
big enough for a hospital bed, Hoyer Lift, wheelchair, and medical
supplies. Fortunately, our house was a one-story ranch style.

It had a large living room with easy access in the center of the
house. The living room was by the front door and had never had
much furniture in it. In the past I had used it for Tai Chi, dance, Yoga,
massage, meditation, and healing. It was my room and did not have a
television in it, which suited me just fine. Like many men, Mark would

have a television in every room if he had the choice. This room was the only practical place to put Mario

To convert the living room to a bedroom, we took all the books out of a large bookcase and used it for medical supplies. I covered the wall-to-wall carpet with an eight-by-ten carpet sample I had used in my classroom. That was good thinking since there would be many spills, from urine, liquid food, and vomit.

We started our preparations immediately. We had only two weeks to get ready. Mario was coming home January 30th. Mark built three sturdy ramps. As usual, he built them to last. I thought it was over-kill at the time. I remember thinking we would only need them for a year or two.

Our house has a beautiful view of Mt. Diablo and offers lots of natural sunlight. It has large sliding glass doors and windows, which made easy access. If you were going to be confined to a house, you couldn't pick a nicer one.

We were so grateful to have a one-story ranch style home. A two-story apartment or house with lots of stairs would have been almost impossible. These are things you don't think about when you are young and healthy. Now I would never choose to live in anything but a one-story.

The spring before Mario's accident we put in a beautiful pool with a beach landing and cement patio. The old wooden deck would have been very difficult to get Mario on. The pool is on a hillside and there are many steps down to it. We would have to build a trail around the side of the house to get Mario down to the pool.

The pool was another blessing. It was in that pool that we were able to get our first leg movements from Mario. It was also in the pool that we got Mario to stand up. We asked our HMO for a standing frame, but it took one year before we received one.

It would still be many months before we could bathe Mario. He would have to be content with bed baths until we could get a wheelchair accessible shower made. As for toileting, Mario came home in diapers, with no bowel or bladder control. We'd be starting from scratch with that one.

I remember that when the hospital bed arrived I was horrified, because it was a standard hospital bed with a hand crank to raise and lower it. Why wasn't he getting the fancy airbed that adjusted his position, like the one he had been in at the rehab center, nursing home, and hospital? That bed had an electric motor to raise and lower it.

I called the HMO to complain. I was told that it was the standard bed sent home with all patients. Mario was not an exception. What you see is what you get. It was not a comfortable bed, but what more could I do? We were being burdened with all kinds of extra expenses, so renting a nicer bed was not practical.

When we went for our training on caring for Mario, we took Mario's friend Stephanie with us. She would be the first of many caregivers and started out working five days a week with Mario.

Stephanie was a young mother of nineteen. She and her husband were struggling to make ends meet. It was her dream to become a nurse. Her daughter was only two, and on many days, she brought her to work. Later we would recruit more friends to help on the weekends with Mario. Mario's girls would all rally to help us.

Because Mario was an adult, he qualified for two hundred and eighty-three hours a month of in-home support services. We would get money from the state to pay someone for Mario's care. The caregivers got a whopping $8.50 an hour, with medical benefits, if they worked at least eighty hours a month. Today they get $10.50 an hour.

Private agencies charge twenty dollars an hour to care for someone as needy as Mario. That was something we could not afford. Where would we have found help to care for Mario at that low wage if he had not had friends?

We were so blessed to have someone like Stephanie. She not only cared for Mario, but was dependable and loved Mario as a dear friend.

At the training we all learned how to change Mario's bed and how to bathe and dress him. This was no easy task. At least Mario was lightweight. He came home to us weighing only one hundred and twenty nine pounds.

We learned how to put a condom catheter on his penis and attach it to a Foley bag or leg bag. The leg bag was used when he went out of the house or to classes. The Foley bag was used while he was at home or in bed. We had to be trained on how to use a Hoyer Lift to get him into a wheel chair and in or out of bed. Then there were the exercises and braces that had to be taken off and on several times a day.

Caring for Mario was a full time job. When the nurse told us we would have to change Mario's body position once every two hours, even at night, I rebelled. I told her that there was no way that I was going to get up every two hours each night to change his position. I needed my sleep if I was to function in the everyday world. With my job as a teacher, I just couldn't afford to deprive myself of sleep, by having to get up every two hours. Once I explained this to the nurse, she conceded and said every four hours should be good enough.

The reason they wanted Mario moved so often was to prevent him from getting bedsores. These ulcers can be deadly for people who are wheelchair or bed bound. Mario had experienced one on his heel from the stay in the nursing home.

We even had to learn how to give Mario a shot each day in the stomach! Stephanie and Mark both administered shots, but again I refused. Another fun task was learning to apply a suppository in his rectum. After many months of doing this, we discovered that a glass of prune juice every day was just as effective. No one told us about prune juice; we just figured it out on our own.

Feeding Mario was easy at the rehab center, but hell at home. While at the center, he was on a continuous feed with a drip line. We simply inserted the line into his feeding tube, flushed it with water, got all the air out and filled the bag with food. It would empty into Mario's stomach in about two hours. Once he was home, he was set up for bolus feeding. Mario came home January 30, 2003.

It was the bolus feeding with a syringe that was challenging. With bolus you fill a syringe with food, attach it to the feeding tube and slowly push the food into Mario's stomach. What was so hard about that? Mario did not like being fed this way and would try to pull the tube out by grabbing it with his left hand. You had to try and hold Mario down, stick the syringe in the tube and push the food into him while he fought you. It got so difficult that we had to put mittens on his hand and tie his arm down. Not a fun job.

Stephanie deserved combat pay to work with Mario. Each feeding took about ten minutes using four syringes. If we fed Mario too fast he would vomit the whole mess up and you would have to clean him and try again later. The feeding tube was the only way Mario got any liquids or medications into his body. When he vomited his medications, we never knew how much we should give him the next time around.

All the medications had to be ground up before putting them into his feeding tube. It took about forty-five minutes just to grind up all the pills he had to take. This had to be done four times a day! After a week of grinding, my husband got the idea of using a mortar and pestle. With this simple tool it took less than a minute to crush all of Mario's medications. Why hadn't somebody told us? We were so overwhelmed with the level of care that Mario required, that even figuring out simple procedures often eluded us. All I could do was pray for the courage to go on. I don't know how Mark coped, but he did.

I also prayed that my back would hold up. I have suffered with chronic back problems since the age twenty-one. I had hurt my back from falls off horses and have always babied it, careful not to lift too much. I have been faithful about doing my stretching exercises every morning to keep it flexible. Would this extra demand be too much for my back?

Mario slept OK the first night. I moved him before I went to bed at 10:00 p.m. and Mark moved him before he went to bed at midnight. Then I got up at around 2:00 a.m. to move him again. I am an early riser, so I moved Mario again at 6:00 a.m. He never went more than four hours without having his position changed. It turned out that Mark staying up late and me going to bed early worked out beautifully.

Stephanie came in at 8:00 a.m. and we were ready to start the day. This is what she wrote on that first day:

"In the morning you ate, Mario, then you threw up. I took you outside and I was sitting by you. When I got up you picked up my chair with your right arm! You got some healing from your mom and her friend, Virginia. It seems as if whenever you eat and get your medicine you start sweating and get mad. I love you, Mario!"

Having Mario home was no picnic. Dr. K had been right to encourage us to take a vacation while he was at rehab. We would be house bound for the next eight months! No more horse camping or weekends away in our Lance camper. It was like having a newborn baby, except this one was not only in diapers but weighed one hundred and twenty nine pounds. Mario baby would scream and yell, but could not be picked up and comforted.

Communication was and still is our biggest challenge. It was always a guessing game to try and figure out what was bothering Mario.

We would have to ask questions and try to get a response with a raising of the arm for yes or a head shake for no.

Mario, are you in pain? Does your stomach hurt? Do you have a headache? Are you thirsty? Are you hungry? I eventually knew which set of questions to ask on a regular basis.

I recently asked Mario if he remembered pulling out his feeding tube all the time? He said yes.

I asked him why he did it. "Didn't you want to live? Or were you just mad?" Mario wrote on his computer that it itched! The poor guy, we never would have guessed that. If we had known maybe we could have put some anti-itch cream on or given him some Benadryl, but how were we to know? These were very frustrating times for all of us.

CHAPTER 21

Starting Over

Ask me a question. Anything you want... I'm an open book for this life is just a coloring book made in Braille for a blind man to figure out... Although we may get outside the edges at times, nobody can critique us or say it is easy.. There are no mistakes in life... Only various paths lead by our weightless footsteps... Let you lead the domain of your labyrinth... Never stop to wonder if it's too late or the road seems too long for there is no map or right way to get to where we feel we need to be... Take a chance... A leap of faith... Do not piggyback on others' dreams... Take life into your hands and make it happen... All of us are given the right tools and keys... Whether we know how to use them or are too scared to is another story...

Miguel Scharmer

Dr. A from the trauma center had told us that Mario would have a long and difficult recovery.

He said, "It will be like raising Mario again, from a suckling baby to an adult." He said Mario's recovery would take a long time. We had been through the newborn stage, where everything went into the mouth, now we were experiencing the toddler years of the first kiss, the first smile, eating solid foods, and beginning body movements.

Mario's anger rages, however, were more like the terrible twos than a six month old. What were we going to do?

I had started back to work teaching a combination class of second and third graders. These seven and eight year olds were way ahead of

Mario in their cognitive development. Was he going to have to learn everything again? Were all those years of high school education gone forever? It made me sick to think about the waste of his education. He was about to go to college and now Mario wore diapers, couldn't talk, eat, move, or remember!

When we finally got him to respond to yes and no questions, we discovered just how bad his memory was. Mario didn't remember who his friend Stephanie was. She was caring for him now and had known Mario for three years before the accident. He didn't remember his dogs, Freesia or Mochi. Mario didn't even know what a pizza was!

I didn't know just how hard all this was on our oldest son Miguel. He didn't express his feelings and seemed OK. He shared some of his darkest thoughts with me while I was writing this book. These are Miguel's words:

"The doctor told us that Mario had severe brain damage and more than likely would not have a meaningful recovery. I never cried about it or even got angry or upset. I just ignored my feelings or buried them.

"When Mario came home he couldn't hold his head up and he drooled out of the side of his mouth. To me he looked like someone who was not going to recover. In my eyes the brother that I knew had died. I didn't recognize this person before me and did not know how to converse with him. I felt like an only child. This new Mario was some handicapped,/ retarded, brain dead/ vegetable.

"I had given up on thinking he would get any better. He couldn't even feed himself, swallow, speak, or use the bathroom. He had very little control of anything. He needed a caregiver twenty- four hours a day!

"I felt that if that happened to me I wouldn't want to live like that. I would want to pull the plug. Thoughts started to go through my head like,' Does he want to live like this? Would he rather have died?'

"One night I thought about putting a pillow over his head and just smothering him to death and not telling anyone. I debated in my head about it for a while. I finally came to the conclusion that it was not my decision to make. He was my mother's son and I had no right to take him away from her. I had given up hope, but she still held on."

The Passing of Mochi

In October, three months after the accident, our little dog Mochi had not been eating well. She had been gaining a lot of weight and drinking a ton of water. Mark decided to take her to the veterinarian for a check-up. We didn't expect anything major, but felt a check-up would be a good idea. The veterinarian was going to run some tests and we could pick her up in the afternoon.

That afternoon I got a phone call from the veterinarian. Mochi, my little love muffin, had diabetes! It could be treated with daily insulin shots and careful monitoring.

I was so overwhelmed with Mario, how could I deal with Mochi too? Mochi was thirteen years old and had been with us for nine of those years. She was Miguel's and my favorite dog. She slept with Miguel. Miguel had lost his brother to TBI and now he must face the possibility of loosing his dog too. We had two choices, put Mochi down, or take daily blood tests and give her insulin injections. It would prove to be a difficult decision to make.

I made my decision: Mochi would have to go. I talked it over with Miguel and he agreed.

I told the veterinarian, "She is thirteen years old, I have an injured son in the hospital, and so we have decided to put Mochi to sleep. We simply cannot take care of her." I made arrangements to say our goodbyes that afternoon. Miguel went with me.

When we got to the veterinarian we held Mochi in our arms and gave her a dog treat. She was so happy to see us and wagged her tail and licked our faces. Little did she know it was her last greeting.

She loved unconditionally. Mochi loved people and was not afraid at the veterinarians like many dogs. The veterinarian asked if we would like some time alone with her. We nodded yes. It was a very emotional time for both of us. I cried when I told Mochi that she was a good dog and that we loved her very much. Miguel kept petting her as I talked.

I explained to her that she was sick and it was time to release her body. She licked my face more. I sent Miguel in to get the veterinarian. The veterinarian came in, and as I sang sweet songs to her and cried a flood of tears, as she gave Mochi her final injection.

I have been through the passing of several horses, two dogs, and one human. While very emotional, I am still amazed at the peace and unconditional love that I felt at the time of each passing. When the breathing stops there is a sense of freedom and joy of leaving a body behind.

Martin Luther King's words always come to my mind during this time. 'Free at last, free at last, Thank God almighty I am free at last!' Mochi too was now free.

Miguel and I wrapped her body in a blanket and took her home. When Mark got home from work he dug a grave and we buried our little love muffin in our pet cemetery next to Xochi the dog, Willie the cat, Dennis the bird, Checkers the guinea pig, Mr. Peabody the rabbit, and Myrtle the turtle. I dried my tears and went to see Mario. Thank God I hadn't had to say goodbye to him too.

After six months Mario still didn't know what a pizza was. I remember telling him once after he had pulled out the feeding tube that he could get it removed permanently when he could eat a pizza.

He gave me a confused look and I asked, "Do you know what a pizza is Mario?" He shook his head no. I then found a picture of a pizza and showed it to him. Later we brought a pizza home and let him smell, see and taste a little on his tongue. He still couldn't chew or swallow.

The speech teacher at the rehabilitation center had me laminate pictures of our family, friends, events, and pets for Mario to identify. For homework, we used to hand them to Mario one at a time and say the name. We would also lay out three or four pictures at a time and ask Mario to pick up one. We used this system to teach him to identify toilet, cup, food, book, music, bed, and others. He would always kiss the picture of his bed.

Every day was different. It was a lot of trial and error. When I called rehab for help, there were times when they didn't know what to do either.

That first week I must have called four or five times.

"Mario is vomiting after we feed him, what should we do?" I asked.

"He has diarrhea, could it be the medications?" I questioned.

"He is pounding the rail of his bed, could he be in pain from the medications? What should we do?" I asked. Questions, questions, questions, but no answers.

Mark thought that a part of the problem was his medications and told me to ask if we could reduce the amount. Mario was taking thirty-six pills a day! That would upset anyone's stomach.

I asked Dr. K. which ones we could try cutting back on. We decided to use Ibuprofen for pain on request only. Ibuprofen is notorious for causing stomach pain. We also reduced the amount of his other medications. This seemed to help. God bless Mark for coming up with a solution.

Some Helpful Tips

Remember to always ask about drug reduction. You have to experiment with what works and doesn't work. Keep communication open and try to start only one new medication at a time, so you can test results. Keep a chart on bowel and bladder activity. Observe behaviors that you are concerned about so you can track changes. Sometimes it takes weeks before you get side effects from a drug. Even herbs and natural supplements can cause side effects.

Mario gets strange and unusual side effects because of his brain injury. Paxil, a behavioral drug, gives him muscle tightness. After three weeks on Paxil he got so stiff he could not walk with his walker. Omega-3 fish oil makes him incontinent. Ambien causes him to hallucinate, and he doesn't get sleepy. Be careful about what you put into the body, even if it is natural. Everyone is different and what might be a wonder drug for one person may be poison for another. The same is true for other therapies like acupuncture, chiropractic, and hypnosis.

During Mario's recovery we tried many different healing modalities. Each one, or perhaps the combination of them, has contributed in varying degrees to his continual improvement. He now receives acupuncture, chiropractic, and massage twice a month. He goes to the YMCA three times a week to exercise on machines and do pool therapy. At home he does floor exercises.

Every six months he goes to be evaluated by his rehabilitation doctor. She is always interested in the various alternative healing methods we use on Mario.

She will ask, "Do you really think acupuncture is helping Mario"?

I respond by saying, "Dr. K, Mario keeps getting better. I think it is because of everything that we are doing for him. Acupuncture is just one of the therapies that is a vital part of his healing."

Because of our communication and his continued improvement she keeps writing referrals for acupuncture and chiropractic treatments.

In February, six months after his accident, Mario got his first massage on a massage table. We were able to move him to a face down position on his stomach. This was not an easy task. Mario's brain was contracting his body forward. He was as stiff as a board and had not been on his stomach since the accident. We had to carefully place pillows under his stomach, and he could only stay face down for a few minutes. He would only tolerate a light touch.

This is what Barb, his massage therapist, has to say about Mario:

"Working with Mario in the beginning was a little like working with a plank of wood, he was so stiff. He couldn't tolerate very much touching or pressure. He didn't like to be stretched or pulled. If I did this, muscles would just tighten up further. So we started with toning.

When I tone, I cup my hands and make a resonating sound with my voice while placing my hands on various parts of his skin surface. The toning vibrated him and seemed to soften him without using any pressure at all. It's a little bit like getting ultra sound without the ultra! I remember thinking that cranial sacral therapy might be good for him because it is so gentle. It works on the core of you and not on the skin, which was so sensitive for Mario.

We introduced Mario to cranial sacral therapy as quickly as we could. He seemed to go deeply into a meditative or relaxed state whenever I worked with his head.

Cranial sacral therapy works with the tone in and around the spine and head in a gentle, gentle way. It is really listening to the body and finding out which way it wants to move. You don't do anything obvious. I am there to assist in the movement and use my energy to help him move in the direction that his body wants to go.

We really don't force the body with cranial sacral therapy. The entire body works on a system where it rotates inward and outward. It inspires like breathing in and expires like breathing out. The entire body responds to the rhythm of the fluid moving inside the brain and spinal cord. It is an enclosed hydraulic system that runs your very core mechanisms. We got to this very quickly with Mario and he loved it, especially the head. Working with his longer torso and spine, he was able to relax without me having to do any pushing. In this therapy we never use more that five grams of pressure. That is a much as a nickel weighs.

Over the past five years there have been a lot of changes. We went from very gentle internal work with the cranial sacral therapy and the toning, and moved into a nurturing mode. I started stroking and patting like a mother would touch a child or you would pet your dogs. I would apply lotion in a very gentle loving way in order to get him used to being touched and get his skin and muscles to move.

After cranial sacral therapy, he was not as resistant to being touched. He was very soon able to tolerate some soft tissue manipulating. This then led to Mario being stretched, moved, and finding his range.

In some cases, such as his right arm and hand, he couldn't move far. But with a little bit of concentrating we found if he put his attention on things and thought about his arm, he could get it a little straighter. If he thought and focused on his hand, he could help his own range improve. I think he learned how to work with his own body. He has had to learn the difference between tightening and loosening.

It has taken some years for him to learn this. His left big toe being contracted up is something else we worked on. Eventually we learned to laugh about it. Once he learned that it didn't have to be work, but play, he had an easier time of it. 'Mario, that toe is creeping up again! Soften it and make it relax and go down,' I would say.

Now after five years, Mario is in charge of his massage. Mario wants certain things and he lets me know. Sometimes by frowning, if I leave a body part too soon. If I leave from massaging his neck, he takes his eye pillow off and looks at me, and I know to come right back and finish that neck. He will point to body parts and he will lift his leg. He will take his pajamas off so I can actually rub his muscles and soften them physically. He now likes really deep work. He tells me so in ways that are not vocal.

Mario has taught me a lot about how to handle people gently. He pretty much taught me patience. He increased my knowledge of my training, like in cranial sacral therapy and toning. He taught me more about my business than any single person on the planet.

He taught me how to work with people, how to ask for permission to do things. The very idea of having to work on someone who could not tell me things was very foreign before I started this. He has improved my training. He has improved my life. He is a joy to work with. It is so wonderful to *see the smile on his face when I walk in the door. He can beam from ear to ear. It is grand to be kissed and hugged by Mario. It is really rewarding. It makes it not work. It makes it fun. It is satisfying in a different way."*

Being Mario's mother has allowed me to interact with and interview a number of people who have been incredibly influenced or changed because of their experience of knowing Mario.

I used to feel so sad about what I thought was Mario's wasted life. What I have learned from going through this experience is that no life is a waste. Now I see how Mario has touched so many people in a different way than he would have had he not had the accident.

Barb responded to my comment by saying. *"I have learned so much from him. He is very valuable to my life experience."*

Chapter 22

Anger and Frustration

I found my peace through appreciation and love for myself and love for the people I'm with. I am showing it everywhere I go. Through that love I have great days. Appreciation for me is for eating, fresh air, love, music, and nature, hearing, seeing, moving, touching, feeling, smelling, tasting, thinking, and living.

Mario Scharmer

Mario's progress was slow and steady. Each week he would accomplish some new task. What was frustrating was the mood swings. He could go from an angelic state to one of demonic rage in seconds.

Even to this day Mario can go into rages over what is to us "small stuff." Ninety-eight percent of the time he is great, but that other two percent can be frightening. We have had caregivers quit because of his behavior. What causes Mario to get so upset?

It is important to know that before the accident Mario was a very controlling type A personality guy. He wanted to make all the rules and rebelled against anyone trying to control him. As a teenager this created a lot of conflict. Things had become better among all of us in the family after his graduation from high school, but at his core he remained a rebel.

Mario was also tidy and organized in his room. Everything was neatly put away in its place. When Mario was a little boy he wanted his food to be placed on his plate " military style." The vegetables, fruit, and main dish separate from each other. It upset him to have any of his food touching. He would refuse to eat if the plate was not set up in this way.

After the accident Mario was put into a helpless condition with very little control of his life or body. Unable to move his body and communicate must have been a living Hell, especially for a youth in transition to manhood. After he began to recover, his behavior became obsessive and compulsive.

Today Mario continues to display signs of obsessive-compulsive disorder. When he uses the urinal, he wants to weigh it and see how much urine was produced before it is emptied. When he has a bowel movement he has to inspect and flush it himself. If a caregiver forgets and flushes for him, a major meltdown will occur.

After washing his hands in a public restroom he has to wipe the counters down before leaving. When he dresses, he must kiss each foot before putting on a sock or pants. He kisses each hand before putting on a shirt. After eating, Mario kisses the plate before you remove it from the table. He will not waste anything and has to have every speck of food eaten before you clear the plate. Trying to clear the plate before each drop is gone will put him into a rage. It is something you do not want to experience.

He even demands that orange peels be recycled and not put into the garbage. On July 11, 2006, a caregiver wrote:

"When a picnic at the Marina Park was over, I threw the orange rinds into the trash can. Mario sputtered and pointed to some nearby bushes.

"I gave him a pad and paper and he wrote. 'The plants want lunch too.'

"I told him that this was a park and the park attendants didn't want people to put orange peels around the plants. He began to go into stage three rage."

As a part of the behavior management system for Mario, I have the caregivers rate Mario's rages on a one to four scale according to severity. A one is mild irritation and a four maximum intensity. All behavioral outbursts are recorded on a chart. Any number three or four stage rages are put into a journal. We talk about the three and four level rages with Mario at the end of the day when he is calm. The journal is also reviewed at his monthly meetings with a psychologist. By having good communication and monthly counseling we have been able to manage and minimize rages without medication.

When Mario gets into a stage four rage, his face becomes distorted, he sweats profusely, and his legs shake uncontrollably. His face turns beet red, and his blood pressure goes sky high. I was at the hospital once when he had raged about some food. Fifteen minutes after this rage his blood pressure was still high 140/90. Mario went to the doctor that day for a pre-operation checkup before toe surgery. That's when I discovered just how high his blood pressure could be after a rage.

When Mario is upset he wants to move, hit, and throw things. He has hurt himself by punching the wall and tried to hurt caregivers by biting, scratching, hitting, kicking, or running them over with his walker or wheelchair. Mario does "sweat the small stuff" to the extreme.

While on vacation one summer Mario had many stage four rages. Here is an example of one that occurred in a restaurant. Miguel and his friend Kat were with Mario at the time. The outburst was over a bite of food that the waitress removed from the table. The plate that she had cleared wasn't even Mario's, yet he still came unglued.

Mario started kicking the table and trying to throw chairs. He put himself on the floor and continued to kick and scream. This time Miguel video recorded the incident. Later in the day when Mario was calm we showed him the video. He didn't remember any of it and asked why he was so mad. How can you reward or punish someone for behavior that he does when he doesn't even remember it?

I shared my dilemma with a friend, and she suggested that we have Mario name this other self that takes over when he is upset. Mario named it Jorge.

Now when we start to see signs of Jorge appearing, we point it out to Mario and say, "Oh no, Jorge is coming out Mario. Keep him in his cage."

Miguel sometimes kids and says, "Satan get behind me!" Mario laughs and often returns to normal. Sometimes if he goes into a level four rage, we video record the event and show Mario later. Since we have been doing this, the rages have been less frequent and much shorter in duration. We have also explained to Mario that to get a girlfriend he has got to get control over his Jorge or boot him out of his life completely. Mario very much wants a girlfriend.

Mario, Out and About

When you take Mario out in public you are sure of some kind of adventure. People love Mario and usually respond to his open heart.

"Hello, I'm Mario, what is your name?" is his usual opening invitation.

I interpret if they are not sure what he said. Mario gets phone numbers from everyone, even (indeed, especially) the pretty girls.

"Damn!" His brother said once. How does he do it?"

People want to give to Mario. While shopping at a mall with Mario we looked at some Croc shoes. They were forty dollars, more than I wanted to spend. After meeting Mario, the clerk said, "If Mario wants to buy some Crocs I will give him my employee discount."

"How much is that?" I inquired.

"Fifty percent," said the clerk.

We bought the Crocs and the clerk let Mario pick out an emblem for his new shoes. He picked out the 49er emblem, red and black. Red is his favorite color.

While at Unity Church, after watching a special Native American drumming ritual, we met Nicholas. Nicholas was a "Sun Dancer" from the Crow Tribe. He gave Mario a hug and stayed embraced until Mario released him about a minute later. Few people can stand still for a thirty second hug, let alone a full minute.

Nicholas was wearing a beautiful black and red beaded necklace with buffalo bones. He took the necklace off and gave it to Mario.

"This is a healing necklace, and I have worn it for many Sun Dances. I want you to have it," said Nicholas.

He gently put the necklace over Mario's head. Mario was beaming and gave Nicholas another bear hug.

I have learned to give myself plenty of time before leaving church because of Mario's long hello and goodbye hugs and kisses. Church is over at 12:30 p.m. We are not back into the car, ready to go, until 1:30 p.m. It is very frustrating to try to get Mario to leave earlier, so why bother.

Another trigger for anger is rushing Mario. After his accident, Mario began to live much more in the present moment. He did not remember the past and could not focus on the future. This is a very healthy place to be mentally. I, along with most of us, could use a little more living in the present. You cannot change the past anyway. Learn from it, but don't dwell on it. The problem arises when you have appointments to go to and projects you want to finish.

Mario has a lot of therapy and doctor appointments. He moves very slowly because of his TBI. Brushing his teeth could take over a half an hour if you don't help. Mario needs someone to help keep him focused. He has to have help with time management. If you let him, Mario can play in the water, rinsing and spitting for one hour!

Mario has a stopwatch for eating and wears a wristwatch. He can tell time but cannot manage his time. Every day we write his schedule on a grease board with the date, day, month, and year. We ask him how long he wants to do exercises and tell him what time his appointments are. With his involvement, we plan out the day.

Problems occur with keeping him on schedule. One temper fit can throw the entire day off. All day long you have to gently move Mario along. "Mario, it is 10:00 a.m. now, so we need to stop your exercises so you can eat. Come on Mario, let's go."

On a good day it takes Mario four hours to get exercised, bathed, dressed, and fed so we can go out. If we skip his exercises and bath we can have him ready in two hours. This is after seven years of healing.

Eating can take from one to two hours, depending on the type of food. Oatmeal, eggs, and waffles are faster. Chinese food with rice, or meats and salads that require a lot more chewing, take longer.

When we get behind schedule, Mario is rushed. "Let's go Mario. Hurry up, Mario. We are going to be late!" Mario does not do well with the rushing and sometimes explodes. Then we are really late!

Being with Mario is like working with a stick of dynamite. You never know when he might explode. People who see the angelic Mario have no idea what we have to deal with that two percent of the time. It takes extreme patience to work with Mario.

Once when I came home from work, Mario was on the floor with Stephanie. He was sitting propped up with two Yoga balls next to the couch. Mario was stroking Stephanie's face with his left hand. He seemed happy and content. Stephanie said it had been a good day.

This is what she wrote: "Mario was very good the whole day. He helped me a lot. He was very relaxed, and when I wheeled him in after our walk we watched television. He seemed to pay attention. Mario was also giving me lots of hugs."

One night when I was reading a bedtime story to him he demonstrated one of these mood swings. I was reading Mario "The Kissing Hand." I climbed into bed to be closer to him. Getting two people into a hospital bed can be challenging. The rails of the bed had to be lowered on one side. I would snuggle up next to Mario. It was very crowded and not comfortable. He was like a small child and I put one arm around him as I read "The Kissing Hand."

This book is about a raccoon mother who sends her baby off to school for the first time. The little boy raccoon is afraid to go, so she kisses his hand and reminds him that her love will always be with him and that he is never alone.

"When you get scared just look at your hand, feel my kiss, and remember you are never alone," the mother raccoon said. I loved this book and read it to my class the first day of school every year. Even Third Grade students are nervous on the first day, and so was I. This book reminded us all that we are never really alone.

Mario seemed to be enjoying the story and would point at some of the pictures. I felt a tremendous maternal love for him as I read. When I finished the story I closed the book and Mario took my hand and kissed it so sweetly. It was a big smacking kiss and I felt overjoyed. I gave him a kiss and then tucked him into bed.

Next I began to read the affirmations that I always did even while he was in a coma. "Mario, you are getting better and better every day. Mario you are perfect love and no one or no thing in the universe can harm you. Mario you are relaxing your body and healing your brain."

After about the third affirmation Mario pushed me away and hit me with his left hand. I felt crushed. I was trying so hard to help Mario, but he didn't want me to read affirmations to him. Why?

This was not how my life was supposed to be. What had I done to deserve this? Mario should be in college, not living at home, lying in a hospital bed, with a feeding tube and in diapers. It should be my grandchild I was reading to, not Mario. Why was this happening to me?

I felt rejected and didn't want to do this any more. I was tired and overwhelmed with life, but what options did I have? Put Mario in a nursing home or institution and watch him fade away? No, I had to be strong.

Mario now says that he was frustrated and couldn't relax his body as the affirmations suggested. He felt he had no control over the healing of his brain.

Sometimes we would use Mario's anger to help with R.O.M. exercises. Once, after we had been stretching his arms and legs, he broke into a rage and did ten leg lifts with each leg! He usually only did about five.

Mario was angry when he uttered his first words. This is what Stephanie wrote on that day: March 17, 2003. "Mario talked today. I was washing his face and he said 'F-U.' He flipped me off, and yelled so loud. I am happy he's using his voice and right arm. I can't believe it. Friday he wasn't using his voice and now Monday he said words! Today was a good day. Today when I got here I looked Mario in the eye and saw the old Mario, and sure enough he spoke. He did stuff he hasn't done in seven months. I'm so happy. I Love you!"

Mario used his anger to make those words. It is called automatic speech and comes from a different part of the brain. He cussed me out the next day when I was doing R.O.M. The words were so loud and clear that Mark, who was sitting on the couch in the other room, heard them too. We were both overjoyed, but these words did not lead to daily speech. After seven years we are just starting to understand some of his speech. The easiest phases are the greetings and requests. "How was your day?" "I love you." "Can I have some water please?" "What time is it?"

It didn't take long for us to realize that we would need more than one caregiver. The job was demanding and five days a week was more than enough time with Mario. We needed someone to help with the weekends too.

Mario's girls stepped up to the plate. One of the girls, Ana, had been a girlfriend of Mario's in high school. During high school she had been a little wild and defiant, like so many teenagers, so her dad shipped her off to New York to live with an aunt. The teen years had been especially difficult for Ana, because she had lost her mother to cancer a couple of years before Mario's accident. She loved Mario and they had kept in contact while she was away.

Ana had just returned to California when Mario crashed into the traffic light pole. The first time she got to see Mario after three years was in a hospital, incoherent and helpless. We needed a caregiver and she offered to help. Ana was in nursing school during the week, but free on the weekends. What was it like to care for Mario, a disabled person after having been his girlfriend? This is what Ana has to say:

"It had been three years since I had seen Mario. I was living in New York with my aunt. We communicated mostly through letters. We had talked on the phone just three days before his accident. I was excited to see Mario again. I thought we might go out, but I didn't want to be just another one of "Mario's girls."

I called his house and found out what had happened to him. I talked more with Miguel and went to the hospital to see him in the ICU. Mario was hooked up with wires and tubes and not communicating. He was in pretty bad shape. It was really sad to see him that way. I went a couple of times a week to visit Mario and continued to visit him both in the hospital and nursing home. I went to the training Christine had organized, so I knew how to use the sensory kit and do the range of motion that Mario needed. I had never known anyone hurt like Mario and didn't know what to expect. I pretty much thought that he would recovery from his injury. I knew it might take some time.

When Mario came home Christine asked me if I could help care for Mario on the weekends. I had started nursing school and thought the experience would be helpful, and besides, I just wanted to help. It was really hard taking care of Mario. He had been my friend and here he was, unable to talk or do anything to care for himself. I had to change his diapers, feed, dress and bathe him; I even had to use suppositories on Mario so he could have regular bowel movements. He had to be fed through a feeding tube, which he didn't like. Sometimes I had to put mittens on his hands so he could not scratch, bite, or pull the feeding tube out! Once when I was putting his leg braces on Mario kicked me. It was so overwhelming that I broke down in tears. I told Christine that I didn't know if I could continue to do this. I was trying so hard and Mario just didn't seem to care. She told me not to take it personally, that Mario did that to everyone at some time or other. He was just really angry and uncomfortable. I stayed.

Christine asked if it bothered me to have to do all the personal care for Mario. That didn't bother me at all. My mother had died from liver cancer when I was fourteen. She suffered for one and a half years and died at home. Being the only daughter, I took care of her. Taking care of her in turn helped me prepare for later caring for Mario. I had to help her eat, take showers, clean a huge incision from her biopsy, and make sure she took all her meds. It was so hard because I was so young, but what made it even harder was watching her fade away. So doing all that stuff for her didn't bother me, because I knew that she couldn't do it herself and the fact that I was doing whatever I could to make her comfortable as I could also gave me strength. When the cancer completely took over and she couldn't even stand on her own, she would look at me and say, "I can't believe you are caring for me. I'm the mother. I should be taking care of you." I think that's another reason why doing all the stuff with Mario didn't bother me either. I felt so happy to be helping someone. My mother's death made my motherly instincts come through. I wanted to have my own kids to care for and be there for. I guess to fill the void of loosing her.

In 2003 Stephanie his other caregiver got pregnant. She continued to work until January 2004. It became too difficult for her to continue so I took the position. I worked with Mario until the winter of 2004, when I too had become pregnant with my first child, Jayleen. Christine used to tease that Mario was the "God of Fertility."

This experience has changed my life. Mario has made a huge recovery. He has a great frame of mind and is always positive and loving. He still has a long ways to go, but I think he will make it. Now that I am older, I don't go out drinking. I am married with two daughters now. When my kids are in high school I am definitely going to use Mario as an example. I want to instill in them how dangerous driving under the influence can be. I think it is very important for people to take Mario as an example and learn from his mistake. Mario is actually lucky because he didn't hurt or kill anyone else."

Another friend, Amanda, had a husband and baby of her own. She was willing to work as a substitute when Ana or Stephanie could not work. Mario was very cooperative on her first day of work.

Ana wrote: "We started the morning off with a relaxing bed bath. Then we did some arm and leg massages and stretches. Mario was so relaxed he fell asleep. When we got him dressed and in his chair, we wheeled him outside. He sipped some mango juice. He swallowed about five spoonfuls and did not spit any out! Good job Mario! We put a hat and glasses on him to keep the sun out of his eyes. He had his leg and arm braces on. He motioned with his left arm like he wanted them off. We asked him if he did and he nodded yes. 'You don't like these, do you Mario?' When we took off the braces he smiled. It was heartwarming to see!"

One night, just as Mark and I were about to go out to dinner, Mario threw up! He was not a happy camper. Ana and Miguel were going to care for him. I helped get him cleaned up and then we left. We had a much needed night out, but I still worried about Mario. Ana and Miguel knew our cell phone number, so everything should be OK. It wasn't.

Ana and Miguel had placed Mario on the floor with the two yoga balls. When they did some R.O.M. Miguel had teased Mario by putting his big toe near Mario's mouth. Mario bit it:- ouch! Just after they had fed him his evening meal at about 9:00 p.m., Mario reached over and pulled the feeding tube out. They had tried to call us, but we were out of cell service range, so they called 911.

When we arrived home, there in our yard was a fire truck. We rushed into the house to find Mario on the floor with a fireman leaning over him. He had blood on his stomach where the feeding tube had been removed. We told the fireman assisting Mario that this happened all the time and it was not an emergency.

It didn't take long for the ambulance to arrive. Two men came into the house and Mark explained the situation. "This is not an emergency, but we do need transport to the hospital. Mario has pulled out his feeding tube before, but we need to get him to the hospital so it can be reinserted," Mark said.

The firemen left and the two EMTs carefully put Mario on a gurney while I explained to Mario what was happening. Thank God Mario was cooperative and calm.

There was no need for both Mark and me to go, so this time I went alone. We had learned to support each other in this way. Two tired parents were of no benefit to anyone. I could sleep in when a caregiver arrived in the morning.

I kissed Mark goodbye and got into the back of the ambulance and rode by Mario's side. I told Mario's story to the attendant. People were always curious about what had happened to him. I explained Mario's miracle and how he had not been expected to live or recover.

"We have a long ways to go, but we are hopeful for a full recovery," I said.

It was a short ride, only about twenty minutes. There were no sirens, flashing lights, or high-speed maneuvers. All I heard was the hum of the engine and the low vibrations of our voices.

The emergency room was packed. It was another busy Saturday night in the hospital emergency room. I filled out papers and again explained the situation to an intake nurse. Mario's missing feeding tube was not a medical emergency, but if he went too long without his medications, it could turn into one.

We would have to wait our turn, but where? There were no rooms available and Mario could not sit up in a regular chair, so Mario was parked in the hallway laying on the gurney. We waited in that hallway for three hours.

Mario lay comfortable on his gurney while I stood leaning next to his bed. My feet hurt and I was tired.

"Please God, don't let Mario have a spaz attack now! I cannot take much more excitement," I said.

Shortly after my prayers, a doctor came over. He looked at the hole in Mario's gut and said, "This shouldn't take long." He took Mario away and was back in about thirty minutes.

Now we could go home? It was about 1:00 a.m. There was only one problem: the ambulance we arrived in had left, and our HMO didn't want to pay for another ambulance ride back home. We couldn't put Mario into a regular car. He needed transport by bus in his tilt wheelchair, which was at home, or by ambulance in a gurney.

A nurse came over and told me she was having trouble finding transport and we might have to wait until 8:00 a.m. to get one.

"No!" I pleaded.

"We have got to get home tonight. All of Mario's medications are at home and if he doesn't get them soon he could go into a rage. We have been through this before and we were always given transport back home," I pleaded.

The nurse responded with, "I'll see what I can do."

Here we go again, I thought. I took a deep breath, relaxed, and again asked God for help. The nurse came back shortly after my prayers and stated with a smile on her face. "I have found you a transport. It will arrive in about thirty minutes."

I thanked the nurse and filled out more papers for the transport, hoping we would not end up paying for it.

It was about 2:00 a.m. when the ride for us came. Mario had been in and out of sleep and seemed quite comfortable. I was beat. My feet, back, and head hurt. I could barely keep my eyes open. At last the answer to my prayers had arrived.

Another EMT came over to Mario and I told him the story again about the feeding tube incident. I skipped the whole crash survival routine. I was tired and just wanted to get home. The EMT pushed Mario's gurney into the back of the transport. It looked like an ambulance to me; oh well.

As I staggered along ready to get in, I heard a voice. "Mrs. Scharmer! Remember me? I'm Adam from fourth grade," a young man shouted.

"Adam?" I replied curiously. I do remember you. Wow! Can I ride up front with you so we can talk?" I asked.

"Sure," Adam said.

Adam was the ambulance driver. It turns out that when they are not responding to an emergency, they transport people from hospital to home or a nursing home. It was the same vehicle, just with a different name according to its immediate use. I told Mario that I was going to ride up front and that we were going home now. An attendant would ride in the back with him.

As I climbed in next to Adam in the front passenger seat, I was now excited and alert. What a shot in the arm riding next to him was. I will never forget that ride.

Adam was twenty-six years old and had been doing the ambulance thing for about four years. He said I had been his favorite teacher. He remembered fourth grade fondly. He asked me if I remembered the "Cinco de Mayo" dances we did and the monthly visits to a nursing home.

Visiting a nursing home was something I did for the nine years I worked at our school. Adam remembered the "Gold Rush" we had out on the field when everyone had dressed the part of a miner. "I was Jake Digger, complete with boots, jeans, hat and mustache! I made a pretty cute guy if you ask me." Adam talked about the simulated town (our classroom), and how he had learned to balance a checkbook, something that was still useful for him to this day.

It had been fifteen years since I had taught fourth grade and I was flooded with warm memories of it. My teaching had made a difference in this young man's life. That was why I had gone into teaching, to make a difference. Lord knows it was not for the money!

After our trip down memory lane, Adam asked what had happened to Mario. He was so sorry to hear about it and wished us all well. When we arrived at the house he helped get Mario settled into his bed. He offered to give me the blankets they had used in transport. They are just thrown away after each use. I accepted the blankets. I told Adam how meeting him that night was an answer to my prayers.

By the time I got to bed it was 4:00 a.m. I felt renewed and refreshed. I could hardly wait to tell Mark what had happened, but wait I did. Mark was sleeping soundly and had his motor of soft snoring running smoothly. I was grateful I was the one who went to the hospital that night because of Adam. What would be the next big adventure? God only knows.

Life for me is a collection of experiences. Some of them are fun, some horrific, but even during the most challenging events you can experience a miracle and a little bit of joy. You just need to ask for help and be open to receiving it in many different places and forms.

It is through my faith, knowing that I am never alone, that I am carried across the muddy waters of life. My prayers are always answered, and that is what gives me the confidence to keep on going.

CHAPTER 23

Mario Inspires Us to Become More Creative

Stay smiling because a smile is priceless and brightens your day.

Mario

As time went on Mario continued slowly to improve. He was able to roll over from one side to another and turn his head to the right. Mark had gotten very creative with range of motion and was using beanbags to help. He would place a bag on Mario's leg or foot and Mario would kick to try and remove it. Each time the beanbag came off we would replace it. This activity made the work of R.O.M. more like a game.

Another discovery I made was to have Mario pull a rope, hand over hand, while in his wheelchair. I tied a fifty foot rope to our basketball pole out in our front driveway and wheeled Mario about thirty feet away. I would then encourage him to pull himself across the driveway toward the basketball pole using a hand over hand movement. Mario liked doing this, so again we got the exercise and stimulated his brain with a little added fun.

Mario had loved playing soccer as a teenager, so I thought maybe kicking the ball with his feet would be a good idea. Mark or I would roll a Yoga ball to him and he would try to kick it back. He got pretty good at this with his right leg, but still could not do much with the left. It is amazing how the brain works. He could use his left hand but not the right, and his right leg but not the left. His tone was much tighter in the right hand and left foot.

In March, about eight months after the accident, he was able to hold my hand in his. At this time he could eat many soft foods like applesauce, yogurt, mashed potatoes, Jell-o, and his favorite, ice cream. I remember telling him that when he could eat pizza the feeding tube could come out.

To make sure his brain received nutrition, I started him on a dietary supplement. This product is supposed to feed all your cells and help with repairing damaged ones. It cost seventy-five dollars per month retail, so I became a distributor to receive the discounted rate. It is made from milk whey protein and is in powdered form.

My friend Virginia got a kit to make her own whey and gave me some starter. Now, I still get Mario the good nutrition, but without the expense. I love to tell people that I make my own whey. Aren't puns fun! I also keep chickens, so he gets organic fresh eggs, rich in Omega 3.

By March we had changed his feeding schedule from 8:00 a.m. to 9:00 a.m. We reduced the amount of his intake to one can at a time. It was very difficult to get the required eight cans down in one day.

I asked the doctor for a higher calorie canned food. She was able to prescribe 350 cal. cans of food instead of the 250 cal. can we had been using. With less volume we were able to get Mario fed without as much stomach upset. We also gave Mario water through his feeding tube. We carefully monitored his urine output to make sure he was getting enough fluids.

Some days Mario was calm, but on other days he was a tyrant. At one point, he got so hard for Stephanie to handle that we had to order soft restraints so she could feed him. The restraints were soft mittens with Velcro straps. They were not easy to put on, but manageable one hand at a time. After his hands were put into the restraints he had to be tied down to his bed or wheelchair so he could be fed. All this work just to keep him from pulling out that feeding tube.

Each time before we put on the restraints, we would give Mario a choice. "Mario if you let us feed you and do not pull out the tube or fight us, we will not use the mittens. It is your choice." If he started to hit, bite or scratch, on the mittens would go.

Mario was becoming harder and harder to control at night. Sometimes he would spend the entire night pounding the bed and making noise.

I would get up and ask. "Mario, does your head hurt? Do you have a stomach ache? Are you in pain?" He said no to every question.

Little did I know that the feeding tube itched and he wanted it out.

In the morning there would be evidence of Mario's frustration all around his bed. All the blankets and pillows were on the floor. His condom cap and diaper were torn off. His nightshirt and protective Velcro waistband would be undone. If we were lucky, the feeding tube would still be in place. In one week he managed to get to his feeding tube and pull it out twice!

So what did we do? We tried to outsmart the rascal by wrapping him up like a package at night. First we put his Velcro waistband on to cover the feeding tube. Next we put on a tee shirt over the waistband. After that we slipped on a blue suit or Dixie. He looked like he was ready to crawl under a car and do some mechanic work. When the blue suit was zipped up nice and snug we fastened it down with a diaper pin. To make sure Mario didn't get jabbed by the pin we covered it with duct tape. Just to be safe, we also put on Mario's hospital mittens! Houdini would be challenged to escape this!

It took Mario all night, but by morning he would be free. He used his teeth to remove the mittens and his thumb and forefinger on his left hand to do the rest. All this perseverance and effort from what was supposed to have been a vegetable. Mark and I were frustrated, but impressed. What were we to do?

As a last resort we had to get more medication for Mario at night. We needed to sleep and Mario needed to keep the feeding tube in.

By March 28th we had our new medication. It made a big improvement. We still wrapped Mario up each night and continued to do so until his feeding tube was removed for good in November.

It was starting to get a lot warmer by April and I thought it would be nice to give Mario a real shower, but how? Once again we got creative.

In the wintertime we used to have to wash the mud off our horses before riding them. The horses hated cold water so I had learned how to hook the hose up to the bathroom faucet and run it outside. Why couldn't we do the same for Mario? An outside shower should work out fine. We had been given a tilt potty-chair/bathing-chair from our

HMO. All we had to do was undress Mario, wheel him to the backyard and run the hose through the window onto the patio.

It took three of us to coordinate the entire process. One person would stand by the faucet to control the water temperature, while one would scrub. The third person was needed to hold Mario's hands so he could not pull out the feeding tube. At first Mario screamed and fussed, but later he started to enjoy his outdoor showers. Eventually we remodeled a bathroom, making it handicapped accessible.

Sometimes you have to get creative to solve the simplest problems, like crushing the medications, giving a bath, or keeping clothes on and tubes in at night. Talk to other people, join a support group, relax, take a breath, or pray. Answers will always come if you only ask for help and are ready to receive.

CHAPTER 24

Sola, the Therapy Dog

God put me here to spread love and smile. Smiling feels good.

Mario

Sola, our new dog, grew and grew and grew. By April, she weighed in at sixty-five pounds. Today she weighs eighty pounds. Sola is not the little lap dog I had wanted, but you never know what the Universe will provide when you specify your exact need. In my case I wanted, "The perfect therapy dog for Mario at this time in his life."

To our relief, Sola did not chew off his toes or casts. In fact, Sola didn't chew much of anything except her chew bones and doggy toys. She was a good dog and had been easy to potty train. She didn't cry at night and slept with Freesia, curled up on a giant dog pillow. Freesia tolerated her, but made it quite clear that she was still the top dog.

Every morning we used to put Sola up in Mario's bed so she could be close to him. We told Mario that this was his dog. Sola loved being with Mario. He was so full of interesting smells and drool! Sola would wash Mario's face using her long pink tongue.

One day, after Sola had finished licking Mario, he reached over, grabbed her nose, and kissed it. Mario was beginning to enjoy Sola and would often spend twenty minutes or so petting her. Some of his first smiles came while spending time with Sola. Unlike Freesia, our older dog, Sola could tolerate Mario's rough pinching touch.

When Mario grabbed her ear or pulled her leg as he tried to stroke her, she didn't flinch. Most dogs would have snapped or jumped away; not Sola. She was tough and seemed to sense that Mario was not trying to hurt her. She tuned into his heart center, which radiated love for her. It took a special dog to be around Mario, and she was a perfect match.

As time went on Sola learned to run to Mario's side when he got upset about something. Many times her presence was all it took to calm him down. To this day, when Mario gets upset Sola runs over to comfort him.

After that first year, Mark and I were desperate to go camping again. For the past fifteen years, horses and horse camping had been our major source of recreation. We went horse camping just about once a month. We went to the desert in the winter and places like Point Reyes, Tahoe, and Big Basin in the summer. Our favorite activity was exploring a new trail in the mountains. I often said that I would rather go horse camping with Mark than take a trip to Hawaii or go to Europe! We had not been camping since Mario's accident in August. It was time to go again, but this time with Mario!

Camping With Mario

How were we to go camping with someone as disabled as Mario? We had a truck and Lance camper. The camper was fine for two people, but very cramped with three or four. Besides, it would be next to impossible to move Mario around in a camper or even get him in one with the steps being so steep. We needed something bigger, with easy access and a bathroom. We didn't want to go back to poopy diaper days.

We talked with the P.T. at rehab about camping with Mario. She suggested getting a van with a wheelchair lift. Yuck! Neither Mark nor I wanted to camp in a van, so this was out of the question. We started looking at recreational vehicles. We decided to sell the truck and camper and try to find a twenty-two foot RV with a couch that we could make into a bed for Mario.

We found a used twenty-two foot Mini Winnebago. We took Mario with us to see if we could get him in. With Mario seated on the first step, Mark pulled him up to the second. Mario helped by pushing with his legs. Once inside we stood him up and had him take a few steps to the couch, holding our hands. It worked! Our first big trip would be a week at Yosemite. Were we out of our minds, camping with Mario?

Packing for a camping trip with Mario was an experience. I had to remember so much because of all his special needs. I packed his Foley bags, condom caps, urinal, braces, bathing chair, wheelchair, walker, yoga ball, orthopedic pillow, eye pillow, headphones, medications, and lots of extra clothes in case of accidents. We also took our bicycles and Sola. By this time, Freesia had passed.

Before we left for Yosemite I had purchased a dog harness and trained Sola to pull the wheelchair. We gave Mario a handle like a ski rope to hold onto while Sola pulled. Mario was good at holding because of the early days at rehab. Back then we had trained him to hold on while we pulled him around the hospital. We had trained Mario well.

It took two people to do this safely. One person guided the wheelchair to make sure it didn't fall over in a ditch or off a curb. The second person put a leash on Sola to show her the way and make sure she stayed on task. You wouldn't want Sola to run after a rabbit or squirrel while she was hooked up to Mario's wheelchair.

We went all over Yosemite Valley with Sola pulling the wheelchair. No horses, but we did take our bicycles. We had a wonderful time.

How can you not have a good time in Yosemite? It is such a spiritual place and very handicapped accessible. All the valley trails are paved and cars for the disabled are allowed in places where you normally have to walk, bike or take a shuttle bus. It got cold and even snowed a little, but we were quite comfortable in our little RV, because it had a heater.

When we stopped by the visitor center and Miwok Village, I asked the ranger if Sola could go in pulling Mario's wheelchair.

She said, "No problem."

Mario kissed her hand and Sola got a pat on the head. Sola became Mario's unofficial "therapy dog." I never did get her certified; who had the time to do that? Yosemite Falls is now wheelchair accessible too. This is a great place to visit. Everyone there was very helpful.

"Mario, do you like camping?" I asked. Mario nodded his head yes, pointed to his nose, and took a deep breath.

"Oh you like the fresh air," I inquired. Mario again shook his head yes. Even when Mario was a little boy he would always sleep with a window open because he liked the fresh air. We take Mario to Yosemite every year now.

By summer of the second year, Mario was using a platform walker and could walk about fifty feet. It was slow, but it was still progress. He was eating everything by mouth and no longer had a feeding tube. His speech was still hard to understand, but he didn't drool so much.

Our first horse camping trip was to Big Basin's Rancho Del Oso about thirty minutes south of Santa Cruz. We had been camping at this spot for the past ten years and knew they did not allow dogs. After our warm reception with the ranger at the Miwok Village in Yosemite, I decided to ask the park ranger if we could bring Mario's therapy dog, Sola. I explained that she was not a registered therapy dog, but did pull his wheelchair. He said we could bring the dog.

Rancho Del Oso is a primitive camp and has no showers or flushing toilets. We would need our Mini Winnebago. Now I not only had to pack for us, but the horses too! This took a lot of planning. Mark and I compiled a camping list of horse stuff, Mario stuff, dog stuff, and our stuff. By keeping a check-off list we usually managed to remember everything we needed.

Our new care giver, Maria, had never been camping or horseback riding before. With us she got to experience both. Over the past five years we have taken Maria and Mario to the mountains, ocean, desert, and Yosemite. She has learned to bike, ride a horse, and kayak. Yosemite is her favorite place.

Taking a shower at Big Basin was done in our horse trailer. We pulled the mats back, put a shower chair down, and used an extension for the RV's outside shower. We had a water heater, so at least the showers were hot. We usually took only one shower each on a three-day camping trip. Water was in short supply.

One of the best things for Mario at Big Basin, besides lots of fresh air, was the road to the beach. While it was not possible to take him down to the sandy beach, he could travel the road to the parking lot above the beach and watch the waves, birds, surfers, and kite boarders. It didn't seem to bother him that he could not be active like the young men and women on the beach. He was just so happy to be alive and grateful to be out in the fresh air. Later we bought him a kite, which he enjoyed flying.

The road from the campground to the beach was about a quarter of a mile, so we hooked up Sola to the wheelchair and off we would go. The road is lined with wild flowers and you can hear the roar of the ocean and smell the sea air.

Little bunnies, especially at dusk, hopped across the road. Sola would get excited about the bunnies, but if you just reminded her to "leave it!" she would maintain discipline.

Passersby would comment on what a nice dog Mario had. It was a beautiful thing to see Mario so happy. Whenever we went to Big Basin with Mario, we made sure he got to go down the road at least once a day. Sola made it a lot easier, because we didn't have to push the wheel chair all the way.

By Mario's third year of recovery he was able to walk to the beach using a platform, four-wheel walker. Sola doesn't need to pull him in a wheelchair any more, but she still continues to calm him down when he gets angry or frustrated. Sola is a hero in my book. She was and is the "perfect" dog for Mario.

CHAPTER 25

Here Comes The Judge

Here I wait, no faith in fate, this life I no longer celebrate.
I can't help to anticipate.
Will I be judged before the gate?

Miguel Scharmer

Besides dealing with all the daily chores of working and attending to Mario, we had legal issues to deal with. Mario had been driving under the influence and it didn't take long for him to get a court summons.

The first summons came a couple of months after the accident, while Mario was still in the hospital. What were we to do? It was obvious that Mario couldn't go to court. He was in a persistent vegetative state!

Mark and I decided to get a note from his doctor stating the severity of his condition, which we would take to court. I planned for a substitute teacher and took the day off. Mark changed his schedule so he could go with me.

If you have ever been to court you might have noticed that all the cases requiring a lawyer are the first to be reviewed. I was annoyed that we had to wait almost two hours for our 2:00 p.m. appointment. Later I realized that this was fair and just. Why? If you are paying a lawyer $300 to $500 an hour, you do not want to be paying for wait time.

While a little annoying to Mark and me, it was not costing us a fortune to be there. However, it wasn't fair for us to have to clean up Mario's mess. Thank God he was only being charged with a DUI and not for wrongful death or involuntary manslaughter.

Remember, Mario's car was full of friends just an hour or so before the accident. He could have easily hit another car, causing death or injury to an innocent bystander.

There were times when both Mark and I thought about just not showing up. What would happen anyway? Mario would probably have a warrant out for his arrest. Oh well. But I am too much of a control freak to have let that happen. Now I kind of wonder about what the outcome might have been had we just let things slide.

Mark and I waited for our turn.

Finally, almost last, the bailiff called out, "Mario Scharmer."

We stood up and explained that Mario was in the hospital and unable to come to court. I told the judge that he had TBI, was in a vegetative state with a poor prognosis of recovery.

I approached the bench and gave the judge the report from the doctor confirming what I had said. The judge looked at the papers. The judge asked the D.A. what he wanted to do. The D.A. wanted to prosecute. The judge said come back in six months.

We were all praying for a speedy recovery, but at that moment I was hoping we would not have to deal with a DUI. Mario had been punished enough.

Time flew by and before we knew it six months had passed. It was almost summer when we got another court summons. Mario was home raging, pulling out his feeding tube, and slowly recovering.

He went to the rehab facility as an outpatient every Friday, so getting another letter from the doctor was easy. By now I had started going to rehab with Mario and his caregiver every Friday. I had earned enough sick days to allow me to work a four-day week for the next two years. By the time I retired, I only had five sick days remaining. Still, when the summons came I couldn't help but think, oh no, here we go again.

I took another day off work and this time Mark stayed home. It was warm out and his business was getting busy. I didn't mind, since I already knew the routine. This time there were not as many lawyers and I only had to wait one hour. The same judge was proceeding. A middle aged man, portly, fair skinned, and balding.

" Mario Scharmer," the bailiff called.

" I am here for Mario. He has TBI and cannot talk, walk, or communicate. He is on a feeding tube and it is difficult to transport him. I am his mother."

The judged asked if Mario was getting better. I explained that his recovery was slow and I had a doctor's report. I approached the bench and handed the report to the judge.

" He doesn't even remember the accident and it took him four months to remember what a pizza was." I explained.

Again the judge asked the D.A. if he wanted to drop the charges. The D.A. said "no." Again, the judge said to come back in six months.

I couldn't believe it. What an asshole the D.A. was. Hadn't Mario suffered enough? Besides, couldn't he see that it was the family that had to come to all the court dates? There were no other victims, so what was the point of prosecuting Mario?

I was in a rage when I left. I felt bitter and decided all D.A.'s were assholes. I called Mark and told him what had happened. He too was fired up.

"Next time we go to court we will take Mario with us," Mark said.

That was a great idea. We should have done that sooner. Maybe if they saw the real deal they might have some compassion.

A year and a half after his accident we went to court for the third and final time. Mario was in a wheelchair with a drool towel and condom catheter and leg bag. He was able to eat solid food by now, but still had trouble communicating. He couldn't write yet and we didn't have the Dynavox communication device. I had taught Mario some baby sign language and he could use thumbs up for yes and shake his for head no.

Mark, Maria, and I all went to court. Again we waited. After about an hour, Mario got uncomfortable and started fussing, banging the arm of his chair and moaning. We had Maria take him outside to feed him some yogurt, empty his Foley bag, and let him stand for a bit. The D.A. passed Mario on the way to the courtroom.

"Mario Scharmer," the bailiff called.

"Just a moment your honor. Mario is outside with his caregiver. We will bring him in," I said.

Mark went out to get Mario and Maria wheeled him up to the stand.

"Your honor, I am Mario's mom and his dad is with me. This is the third time we have been to court. Mario is suffering from TBI. He cannot speak or walk. It has been one and a half years since his accident. His recovery has been very slow. As his parents, we are pleading with you to drop the charges. Mario has suffered enough and by continuing to summon him, you are punishing us, his parents, not him."

The judge asked the D.A. if he wanted to press charges?

The D.A. said "yes."

The judge asked the D.A. if there were any other victims in the accident.

The D.A. said "no". The judge then said that it was clear to him that Mario could not go to traffic school or even understand the charges, so he would drop the case. The D.A. then stated that for the record he wanted it noted that he wasn't in agreement.

The judge then called us up to the bench and told us how sorry he was for our loss. He had a brother that had suffered from TBI and was eventually institutionalized. It had become too difficult for his parents to care for him. We thanked the judge for his compassion and left the courtroom with a bittersweet taste in our mouths. While the judge had been compassionate, what was wrong with the D.A.? My feelings about the D.A. are still full of negative judgments. I need to work on that one.

One thing that I learned from this experience is to personalize situations. Whether you are going to court or working with hospitals, Social Security, Medicare or Medical, you have got to get past the impersonal phone calls, names and numbers. Once you do make contact, be polite, loving and kind.

Now we always take Mario with us to any important meetings, even if it would be easier to leave him at home. People respond in a more positive way once they meet Mario and see what we are dealing with. If we had left Mario home that day, I am not sure the judge would have dropped the case.

Chapter 26

Time for Sports

May the Divine Presence in me challenge my being to
broaden the horizon of my beliefs.
Push my life into greater strength, courage, love, and
unity.
May I challenge myself to fearless adventures and new
dreams, based in the love of my being.
May I choose joy, balance, peace, humor, strength of
being, wisdom, and mastery of self.
Giving thanks, for all the days of my life.
And so it is.

Quote from the Divine Source

Row, row, row, your boat gently down the stream, merrily, merrily,
merrily, merrily, life is but a dream. How many times has your life felt
like a dream?

You are an actor on the stage of your life. Like an actor you have
many roles to play: villain, hero, victim. So what makes our lives feel
so real? It is our emotions. Without the deep feelings that we have, all
of the drama of everyday life would be meaningless.

It is our emotions that really set us apart from all other life on the
planet. I am not saying that animals don't have feelings, but because
they live in the now, they do not hold onto them like people do.
Animals do not hold grudges. A dog owner can beat a dog every day,
yet it will wag its tail hoping for a little love when the owner comes
home at the end of a day.

In my life, I have felt many emotions, and at times so strongly that
I sometimes wondered if they would drown me. Yet even in my most

desperate times, I know that nothing lasts, every thing changes, and I am never alone.

If I remind myself to go with the flow and not fight the emotional current of sorrow, rage, loneliness, or fear, my life is easier.

Mario Loves Baseball

A new development in Mario's life is his interest in baseball. As a young child he played on Little League teams. He asked if he could try to hit a ball. I bought a Wiffel ball and plastic bat. I pitched the ball to him, but because of his slow response time he could not hit it. This created a lot of frustration and Mario ended up throwing the bat to the floor. Six months passed and we tried it again. This time he was successful!

I remembered a disabled young man we had met at the movies. His dad worked at Safeway and had told me about Challenger Baseball for disabled kids. He had given me his phone number in case Mario wanted to try and play. It was time to make that call.

I got Mario signed up with a baseball team, the Diamond Backs. The day of the first game we almost forgot his mitt. Mario remembered it! He would not leave the house without his mitt. I remember getting frustrated because I couldn't find it and didn't want to be late for the game.

"Why does Mario need a mitt anyhow, he cannot field," I thought.

At the game Mario insisted on using his walker to run the bases. We sat him in his wheelchair to bat. The coach pitched the ball. Smack! And away flew that ball. He giggled with joy and ran to first base as fast as he could. He always makes sure that he touches each base with his foot before running to the next base. Most of the players could care less. No one is every thrown out.

Mario loves baseball. Everyone on the teams gets to bat and run bases. There are no outs. Every player gets to bat. If they cannot hit a pitched ball, then they will hit off a tee.

Out on the field Mario cheers for the batters, giving each player a thumbs up. Mario fields the ball from his wheelchair. If the ball rolls toward him his caregiver wheels him over to field the ball. Mario slowly picks up the ball with his mitt and then transfers it to his right hand.

He pulls his arm back, and aims for the throw. After about thirty seconds of preparing to throw he lets it fly. The ball barely makes it to the pitcher. Everyone is patient and encourages Mario. It feels great to see so many children and young adults get to play baseball. Each smiling face is priceless.

I was surprised that Mario liked baseball so much better than bowling. His skills are poor for both activities, yet he loves baseball.

Then my brother sent me an article about Alzheimer patients and golf. Apparently patients who played golf when healthy respond in amazing ways when taken to a golf course to play. The article said that even patients who didn't remember playing, once on the course, became more active and alert. Once they set foot on the green and got a club in their hands, they remembered how to play!

It is a deep, almost cellular, memory that our bodies maintain even when part of the brain is injured and not working properly. Like riding a bicycle. Once you know how to do it, the skills stay, even if you don't ride for many years.

Mario played baseball for about eight years as a child. It was a positive experience and programmed deeply into his being. Bowling was not something he did much before the accident, so it just didn't have the same magical impact that baseball has.

Another activity showing his improved response time has been riding a three-wheel recumbent bike.

At first, I was terrified that he might fall off the road into the curb or crash at a high speed. His vision is compromised and we were not sure if he could use the hand brakes properly. We live on a hill off a long private road. There are only five houses on the street. Fortunately, our end of the road is fairly flat with a gentle slope at both ends of the house. There is a cul-de-sac at one end and the other end declines rapidly from a very steep hill. Some of our horse friends were afraid to drive up the steep road pulling a horse trailer. When we wanted to ride, we would have to convince them that it really wasn't a problem, or meet them in the park down below our hill.

On his first ride we made sure he rode down to the end of the cul-de-sac. Mario looked really cute with his red helmet, special bike shoes, and red and yellow recumbent bike. It took two people to get him on the bike. We stood him up from the wheelchair, had him straddle the pedals and then he slowly dropped to a sitting position.

"Mario, go slow, stay in the middle of the road and use your brakes," I cautioned.

"Remember to stop the bike and please don't go too fast," I said, a little more loudly.

Mario started off slowly, but began to pick up speed as the road sloped down.

" Mario stop!" I yelled.

I ran to keep up with him, and he did stop. He made a nice turn and did not get too close to the edge. Back up the little slope and to our house driveway we went.

Mario had completed one lap successfully! He wanted to go again.

"Okay, remember to use your brakes, stay in the middle of the road, and away from the edge," I repeated.

He completed lap two, no problem. Now the "Nervous Nellie" was ready to let Mario go on his own. Fortunately, with his red flag attached to the bike, we could see Mario and would know if he was doing all right as long as the flag was still up.

Mario took off and I prayed to God that he would be OK. It felt like the first time he rode a two wheeler without training wheels when he was six.

It was time to let him stretch his wings and try to fly. He made the turn at the end of the cul-de-sac and I could see him coming back up the little slope. Beaming from ear to ear, here came Mario. Faster and faster he came, right towards me.

"Is he going to stop, or run me over?" I thought.

"Mario, stop"!" I screamed.

He stopped about five feet before impact. Mario was laughing because he had fooled us.

Now he wanted to go in the other direction. However, that direction is a little steeper, but not dangerous until you get past the neighbors' house.

Mario zoomed down the slope and stopped at their driveway. I ran to catch up and Mario motioned to their front door. He wanted me to ring the doorbell so our neighbor Simone could see him on his new bike. She was home and came out to congratulate Mario on his success. She gave him a big hug and a kiss.

Mario continued to practice biking for another twenty minutes.

After only a few laps he was able to bike in two minutes what took him ten minutes to walk. Now that is progress! After six months of practice, Mario can now bike three miles when we take him out to a public trail.

In the Now

Sometimes, for reasons unknown to us, when Mario goes through a brain change his behavior deteriorates. Some weeks we have more stage four meltdowns than other weeks. Here is what Miguel wrote in the journal about one such episode that happened while he was driving Mario home from his computer class:

"Mario was a jerk today. After class he was flipping out about a water bottle I had left. He said he wanted water, so I handed him a bottle, and he was still yelling, kicking and screaming. He flipped me off and started punching the air and dashboard of the car. He kept this going the whole way home."

When Mario got home I heard the screaming. When Miguel came in to get the wheelchair, Mario started honking the horn. Miguel explained to me what had happened. This was the second level four tantrum in one day.

Miguel went out and brought him in. Mario was sweating profusely and all red in the face. He looked demonic, as though he could have a stroke at any moment. All that anger over a water bottle!

"Mario, what is the matter? Calm down and write to me about the problem," I asked.

He wrote about how "fucking Miguel" would not go back and get the bottle that was left in class.

"Mario, do you know how much gas costs right now? Four dollars a gallon," I explained. "You do not like to waste, right? It would be more wasteful to go back to class and pick up the water bottle than to have driven home. Miguel was almost home. You would have polluted the air and spent money on gas for a half a bottle of water. A water bottle costs about fifty cents and gas costs four dollars a gallon. Miguel was right not to go back to get the water." Mario pointed to his head, calmed right down, and turned back into the happy, loving person he can be.

Miguel was still pissed and I would have been too. Mario can get over stuff in an instant, but we hold onto the emotion. He is in the now, and even though his angry feelings are powerful and scary for us, when he is finished they are gone, over and done with.

The next night we had another meltdown over socks. Mario had been having so much fun riding his bike the day before, that we told him if he finished his dinner by 7:30 p.m. he could go on a bike ride. He started eating at 6:00 p.m. and was all finished by 7:15!

"Okay Mario, lets go on a bike ride," I prompted.

Mark took the bike outside and I got Mario dressed in some shorts. He will not bike in jeans. They restrict his leg movement too much. To save some time I grabbed a pair of black short half socks for his feet. They are much easier to put on than full socks. He started to fuss while putting on the socks and continued after the shoes were on.

"Come on Mario, hurry up, we have got to get going or it will get dark and you will not have time to ride," I protested.

Mark went out and started riding the bike himself, having a fun time as I wheeled Mario outside. By the time I had him out the door he was kicking and screaming and pointing to his socks.

" What is wrong with your socks?" I asked.

He mumbled, "black."

"You don't want the black socks? Mario they were easier to put on. You are only riding a bike. You are not going anywhere, so what is the problem?" I asked.

"Black," he mumbled.

Now I lost it. This was supposed to be fun. I am outside with a screaming maniac when I could be relaxing in front of the television with Mark or reading a book.

"Mario, I am not going to change your socks," I yelled. "You can sit here and be miserable or enjoy riding your bike. The choice is yours," I said.

Mario chose to continue to rage. Matching his anger, I pulled off his shoes and black socks.

"Are you happy now?" I asked. You can ride with no socks," I screamed.

Then I put his bike shoes back on without socks. He stopped me so he could kiss each foot first.

Mario, now calm, was put on his bike. Off he went riding his bike as happy as a clam. Mark and I were still angry. It took us a good hour to get over the incident. I really didn't completely get over it until after Mario was put to bed.

In reflection, I now realize that I chose to stay mad and be miserable. I could have let go like Mario and enjoyed the rest of the evening. Whom did I hurt? Me. I was the one who was punished. Mario was out on his bike having the time of his life.

If we can all learn to release and let go a bit and remember to forgive, our lives will be a lot more pleasant. Sometimes I sing, "Row, row, row your boat gently down the stream. Merrily, merrily, merrily, merrily, life is but a dream." I prefer the dream to the nightmare and just go with the flow. How do you choose to live? The choice is yours.

CHAPTER 27

Disneyland

May I accept the flow of life.
May I be opened, balanced and caring.

Quote from the Divine Source

After two years of camping in our twenty-two foot Minnie Winnie, we decided to upgrade to a thirty foot RV. We needed more room for all of Mario's equipment. Sleeping on top of the cab had become uncomfortable with my ever-increasing back problems. Besides, Mark and I needed some privacy.

Our new RV had slide outs and a separate bedroom. Now I could go to bed early and Mark could stay up reading without bothering me. Mario still had to sleep on the couch, because we couldn't get him up into the cab over bed.

This RV also had a larger refrigerator, bathroom, microwave, and tons of storage space. It was a house on wheels. It was also a brand new 2005 model, so we shouldn't have any problems, right? Wrong, we had problems from the start.

Our first trip was to Disneyland and Death Valley. Miguel came along to help us out at Disneyland. He would fly back after Disneyland, so we would be on our own with Mario in Death Valley.

As soon as we started on our trip we noticed that the new RV made a loud banging sound whenever the road got a little rough or you drove faster than fifty MPH. The noise was annoying, but not a major problem.

When we stopped in Bakersfield for the night, Mark observed that the RV battery was low. Great, it wasn't charging the battery properly. Once in Los Angeles we would have hookups, but what about Death

Valley? There were no hookups there. This could be a problem. We would call the dealer in the morning. Everything was under warranty for the first two years, so at least there would be no extra expense.

The next day I called the dealer and complained about the noise and battery. The dealer told me to bring it in and they would fix everything. I explained that we were on vacation and didn't want to waste our time on repairs. We were then about 200 miles from where we had purchased the RV. I told the dealer that we would buy an extra battery and charge it to them. We would tolerate the noise and bring the RV back in for service when we returned. The man at the other end of the line said OK.

We pulled into Anaheim around noon. After checking in and hooking up, we all took showers. Mario went on a walk with Miguel and Mark and I walked the dog.

This small RV park is across the street from Disneyland. It offered shuttle service into the park for one dollar a day per person. We signed up for the shuttle, thinking it would be easier with Mario than putting him in and out of the car each day. It wasn't easier.

It was Christmas break and Disneyland was having record-breaking attendance. On the first day that we visited, it had sold out by noon. Imagine pushing a wheelchair through the crowded streets of Disneyland. Not fun. Thank God we had Miguel to help. It would have been a nightmare without him.

We got up at 6:30 a.m., hoping to catch the 8:00 a.m. shuttle to Disneyland. I woke up Mario and started making breakfast, a quick protein shake in the blender. Mark did Mario's R.O.M. exercises and Miguel walked the dog. We had to empty the Foley bag, feed Mario, brush his teeth, wash his face, and dress him.

"Come on Mario, eat faster, let's go, we want to get to Disneyland and have fun!" I coached.

Trying to get Mario anywhere that early is a challenge and can be exhausting. If you push too hard he might blow up. That could mean oatmeal all over the walls!

It took Mario twenty minutes to drink a twelve-ounce shake. Now all we needed to do was dress him, brush his teeth, and wash his face.

"Open your mouth Mario, so we can brush your teeth," I prompted.

Brush, rinse, spit, and a drink of water, another ten minutes before we were done.

Dressing Mario takes time too, because he has to kiss each hand before putting on a shirt, and each foot before putting on his socks. It was 7:30 a.m. and finally we had Mario ready.

Oh no, Mario says he wants to poop! We waddle him down to the RV toilet and set him on the pot. It is another twenty minutes before he is finished and his butt is wiped. 7:50 a.m. We have ten minutes to reach the shuttle.

We rush out of the RV, get Mario into his wheelchair, and race to the shuttle pickup spot. We just made it! The shuttle drove up the moment we arrived. Guess what? The wheelchair lift is broken, so we have to wait for another shuttle. Hurry up and then wait, what a bummer.

By the time we got into the park it was 10:00 a.m. and we were exhausted from all the effort. Without Mario, Miguel, Mark and I would have been inside the gates when they opened at 8:00 a.m.

Once inside we cheered up a little, because the lines were getting long, but we didn't have to wait in them. Mario and his family got to cut to the front of all the lines because he was disabled. That was better than FasTrak!

When you see the disabled cut to the front of a line, just remember how much effort it took for them or their families just to get out to an amusement park. You will be grateful for your freedom of movement and gladly let the disabled jump to the front of a line.

The first three rides went well. We went on the Indiana Jones ride, Pirates of the Caribbean, and the Haunted Mansion. After we went on Space Mountain, all hell broke loose.

If you have never been on this ride you should know that it is a roller coaster that moves through the dark. You see stars and planets as you travel at what feels like light speed. You cannot tell when a turn or dip is coming, so it is hard to brace yourself. Miguel rode with Mario. I kept my eyes closed for most of the ride, so I missed all the special effects. I prayed it would be over soon. I did not enjoy this ride.

When Mario got off, he did not look happy. His face was disoriented. I asked Miguel how Mario did. Miguel said that Mario laughed through most of the ride and even held his hands up in the air. Only at the end of the ride did he seem to be bothered.

It was now 12:30 p.m. and we were all hungry.

"Let's go for Mexican food," Mark suggested.

We all agreed that Mexican was a good choice, because Mario could eat cheese enchiladas easier and faster than a lot of other foods.

Off to "Frontier Land" we went. Miguel had only pushed Mario a few feet when down came Mario's feet, stopping the wheelchair and preventing it from moving.

"Mom, Miguel called. Mario won't let me push the chair."

"Mario, let's go. We want to get lunch so we can go on more rides," I pleaded.

Mario motioned that he wanted to eat now! I pulled out a banana from his backpack.

"Here Mario, eat this as we walk so we can have time for more rides." I said.

Miguel went a little further, then wham! Down came the feet again.

"Mario, please stop it, we want to go get lunch. You can eat while Miguel pushes you," I pleaded.

Mario would have none of it. He went into a stage four tantrum right in the middle of Disneyland, "the happiest place on Earth."

People were starting to notice Mario now. Mark wanted to vanish and we were all hoping that people didn't think we had abused the poor little disabled kid. We waited for Mario to calm down. His legs were shaking and his face was red, covered with beads of sweat.

"Okay Mario, settle down. You don't want to eat on the go. We will stop. Now eat your banana so we can go," I said.

It took Mario ten minutes to finish one banana. We waited impatiently.

When we finally sat down at the Mexican cafe for lunch, it was 1:30 p.m. Mark and Miguel ate their lunch in about fifteen minutes. It would be another hour and a half before Mario completed his meal.

Mark and Miguel went on some more rides and then went back to the RV to take Sola for a walk. I stayed with Mario while he ate. They came back for us at 3:00 p.m.

Normally Mario takes a nap at around 3:00 or 4:00 p.m. While at Disneyland, we skipped naptime so we could go on as many rides as possible.

Mario's favorite ride at Disneyland was "Splash Mountain." It is a water ride with animated characters, music and water. You sit in a log, with one person in front of the other as you travel down a log run with rapids, dips and chutes. Briar Rabbit and his friends sing and dance to "Zippity Do Da."

Mario loved this ride and we went on it several times. At the end of the ride you shoot down a waterfall and your picture is taken. When you get off the ride your photo is displayed on a screen for you to view. You may purchase the picture in a little shop for a fee. Mario loves to have his picture taken. When he got off the ride he wanted to buy the photograph on display. Afraid that he might go into a stage four tantrum again, we caved in and bought the photo. Mario has trained us well.

When he was a small child, we would have never let him get away with this kind of behavior. But he is so much bigger and stronger now. "Raising Mario Twice" presented all kinds of new and different challenges.

Disneyland offers musical performances at different times and places throughout the park. On our way to Autotopia, a place where you can drive your own miniature car, we passed a band playing Soul music. Mario wanted to stop and listen.

All of us enjoy Soul music, so we stopped and I asked Mario if he wanted to dance. He did, so I stood him up from the wheelchair. He rested his hands on my shoulders and we danced. Mario actually cued me where to move using his right arm and hand to guide me forward and back. I was thrilled with this development. We had tried to dance before, but he had never guided my movements.

After about twenty minutes of dancing we went to Autotopia. Mario got to drive his own car. Miguel rode with him. It had been three years since he had driven a car. Mario was thrilled and after the ride kissed his Disneyland driver's license.

We didn't stay for fireworks. Mario had provided enough excitement for one day. We were all tired and went back to the RV for dinner. We ordered pizza and I made a salad. We had two more days of Disneyland and then off to Death Valley we would go.

After two days of Disneyland with Mario I was beat. My shoulders ached and I felt tired all over. This was not a relaxing vacation. I was holding tension in my shoulders and neck. It was getting harder and harder for me to stay in the "now." I was starting to get overwhelmed with life and all the challenges Mario presented. Little did I know that in the next forty-eight hours I would be facing a life threatening situation. Goodbye Disneyland and hello Death Valley. I looked forward to the peace and quiet of the desert.

Chapter 28

Fire, Fire, Fire

Life makes no promises.
Let your troubles roll right off your shoulders.
As time falls away choices and mistakes made will
fade.
Let all your regrets wash away leaving your body
cleansed for a new beginning.
The hardest part is over if you let yourself start
again.

Miguel Scharmer

On the way to Death Valley, we stopped at the airport so Miguel could return to his job at Home Depot and his girlfriend Lovely. He was anxious to get back home. Four days of helping with Mario was plenty for Miguel. We appreciated all that he had done and were more than happy to pay for his airfare home. We would not have taken Mario to Disneyland without his help. We hugged Miguel goodbye and headed to Calico, a little historic town in the Mojave Desert. It is about one hundred fifty miles from Death Valley. Again we found a place with hookups for the RV.

That evening while Mario was eating we took Sola on a walk for about thirty minutes. We were never out of sight of the RV, but I still felt a little nervous leaving Mario. Just getting away for a few minutes helped Mark and me recharge, relax, and refresh ourselves so we could continue to take good care of him. Taking care of a disabled person like Mario 24/7 can be exhausting. Time away from him helped keep us sane.

In the morning we went into town and got our picture taken at one of the historic shops. Since it was only a few weeks until our wedding anniversary, we decided to dress up in old style wedding attire. I wore a white lacy wedding dress and Mark put on a suit and top hat. Mario was the best man and also wore a three-piece suit and top hat. We had to lean him up next to a counter so the wheelchair would not be in the picture. The picture came out really cute. I just wished Miguel had been in it too.

However, there was a slight problem. The vender ran out of paper. She would have to mail the picture to us. Maria, the vender, had been touched by Mario and I knew she could be trusted.

I remember saying, "It will be safer mailed anyway since we are traveling and camping. It might get crunched or lost in all our stuff." I had no idea just how much safer it would turn out to be.

While walking around the little town a lady came over to see Mario. She asked if she could do a hands-on healing for him. I said sure. Mario loved the healing and kissed her hand. She told him that she would pray for him. People, wherever we go, are drawn to Mario.

Two old cowboys dressed in western attire came up to Mario. One was about eighty and wore a long white beard, hat, and gun belt. His name was Charlie. He said he was the mayor of Calico. Mario wanted his picture taken with him. We took some shots and then Charlie gave Mario an autographed picture of himself and the rest of the Calico crew.

We were on the road again. The RV battery was still not charging, so we stopped in Barstow to buy another one for backup. We decided to get the Jeep battery tested just to make sure it was good too. We didn't want battery trouble four-wheeling in Death Valley, especially with Mario. That would be a real nightmare. The battery checked out just fine.

The loud banging noise continued all the way to Death Valley because the roads were rough. The music was turned up to try and drown out the irritating noise. At least the CD player worked. Radio reception was poor.

It was getting dark when we pulled into campsite #118 at Furnace Creek. We ate dinner, set the refrigerator to gas, cleaned up, and went to bed.

When I woke up at about 7:00 a.m., the sun was shining and

there was not a cloud in the sky. The weather was beautiful. After my morning meditation and Tai Chi exercises, I woke up Mark. We got Mario up and dressed. Mark did Mario's R.O.M. exercises while I made breakfast. This was going to be a great day!

I made a big breakfast: eggs, sausages, hash browns, and a power shake for Mario. Every day I made sure Mario got his power shake with whey protein. This brain food was supposed to help speed up the healing process. Mark and I finished eating in about fifteen minutes. It would take Mario at least another hour. The plan was to stay in camp, soak up the sun, and relax. We would sightsee tomorrow. We were all tired of driving.

While Mario ate, Mark and I took Sola for a short walk. After twenty minutes we returned and Mario was still eating. What to do now?

"Do you want to go for a bike ride to the store?" Mark asked.

"Do you think Mario will be OK?" I replied.

Mark said, "Yes."

I asked Mario and he motioned for us to go.

"Okay Mario, we will be gone for about twenty minutes. Now remember, stay seated at the table inside the RV," I explained.

Just before we left we had Mario pee in the urinal. I put on some soft, easy-listening music to occupy his mind. I felt a little nervous leaving him, but what could happen? It wasn't like Mario could get up and walk around.

We put on our helmets and mounted our bikes. After Mario's accident we had become very conscientious about protecting our heads while biking or horseback riding.

At the store I bought some postcards and looked around at clothes. They were cute, but too expensive. Ah, but what great hats I thought. On a rack were some very nice hiking hats. Western style, waterproof, and on sale! Now you're talking. I called Mark over and he liked the hats too. They came in green, black, brown, and tan. I liked the brown one, but it didn't have a tag and the clerk wasn't sure that it was on sale too.

"I will have to go in the back and check," she said. "It will only be a minute!"

Five minutes passed and no clerk. What is keeping her so long? I thought. We have got to get back to Mario. Finally the clerk came back. The brown hat was not on sale. Darn! Decisions, decisions, what should I do? Mark helped by suggesting that we buy three green hats, one for each of us.

"Okay, we will take three hats please, but do hurry, we need to get back to our camp," I said.

The purchase was made and back to our bikes we flew.

"Do you want to stop at the stable and look at the horses?" Mark asked.

I am a horse crazy kind of person and almost never pass up a chance to look at them.

"No, we better get back to Mario, it has been more than twenty minutes," I replied.

Now on the bikes we raced back. It was only about a two-minute ride. We came around the corner and Mark saw it first. Thick, yellow/black smoke was coming out of the vent at the top of the RV.

"Oh my God, the RV is on fire!" Mark screamed.

He peddled as fast as he could, dropped the bike, and ran to the RV. When he opened the door all hell broke loose. The flames spread to the ceiling. The ceiling melted and rained hot liquid plastic. It was like Napalm sticking to everything it touched. The smoke alarm was on and there was Mario eating his breakfast, without a care in the world. Sola was sitting in the driver's seat looking worried.

Mark grabbed Mario by the armpits and quickly dragged him out. There was not a moment to lose. Mario's shirt and pants were on fire from the hot melted plastic. I patted the fire out with my jacket while Mark returned for the dog. At this point several neighboring campers had run over with fire extinguishers to try and put out the fire. They were useless. Mark called the dog, but she wouldn't budge. He ran to the passenger door, opened it, and Sola ran out. Mark then shut off the gas and disconnected the power. He really knew what to do in an emergency.

Our years of search and rescue training had really paid off, but where were the fire trucks? It took about fifteen minutes for them to arrive. Death Valley has a volunteer fire department. We were lucky they got there when they did.

We were fortunate that both Mario's walker and wheelchair were out of harm's way. We also had our wallets and cell phones. Our wedding rings, cameras, shoes, clothing, keys, and camping equipment were all in the RV. Would we loose them all?

The firemen quickly secured the scene, moving us back. They wanted us to move the Jeep, but we couldn't find the keys. An EMT began to assist both Mark and Mario, taking vitals and asking questions. Mario's hands were burned a little, but the EMT was more concerned about smoke inhalation. He wanted both of them to go to the hospital in Las Vegas one hundred and fifty miles away! I didn't want them to go. They looked just fine to me.

After about twenty minutes the firemen completely extinguished the fire. They were able to save a lot of our things. We were lucky. One minute longer at the store and Mario would have been toast!

Mark found a set of keys in a jacket pocket, and we moved the Jeep. After a lot of pressure from both the EMT and police officer, we agreed to go to the hospital in Las Vegas. Mark and Mario would travel by ambulance, and I would follow in the Jeep so that we had a way back to Death Valley. But what about Sola, where could she go? We couldn't take her to Las Vegas because we had no idea what we were in for. The police officer offered to take her home with him until we returned. The universe provided again.

Still shaking from all the excitement, I tried to collect my thoughts. Water, wallet, cell phone, purse, gas. Did I have enough gas? Yes, Mark had filled up the Jeep in Los Angeles.

The ambulance was ready to roll. I gave the officer Sola's leash and we exchanged phone numbers. I petted Sola goodbye and started up the Jeep. We had a police escort to the California border. From there Mark and Mario would be transferred to another Nevada ambulance, and then on to Las Vegas.

The police and ambulance traveled between eighty-five to ninety MPH. I had never driven that fast in my life. My shoulders were as stiff as a board and I was running on pure adrenaline. I white knuckled it all the way to Las Vegas, a one and a half hour drive.

Once on the freeway we slowed down to seventy-five MPH. I prayed I wouldn't get pulled over for speeding. I didn't know the name of the hospital we were going to and my cell battery was almost dead.

"Dear God please keep Mario and Mark safe and help me to stay calm," I pleaded. My prayers were both answered.

We checked into the hospital at about 2:00 p.m. Once there,

both my boys were X-rayed and blood tests were ordered. Thank God Mario remained calm during his entire hospital stay. He was hungry and concerned about not getting to finish his breakfast!

While we were waiting for the results of the tests, Mark and I called insurance companies and talked about what might have caused the fire. Mario heard us and motioned for paper. He wrote that he knew what had caused the fire.

"What do you think Mario?" I asked.

Mario wrote, "Lovely was cooking breakfast. That's what caused the fire."

Lovely was Miguel's girlfriend. She had not come on the trip with us and was living in Martinez. What was Mario thinking? Maybe Lovely burns what she cooks! We laughed.

Later we learned that apparently the fire started in the propane refrigerator.

Finally a doctor came in and told us that everything looked good from the test results and Mark and Mario would be discharged in about an hour. We all needed a shower and some clean clothes. We decided that I should go shopping while they waited to be discharged. The closest store was a Walmart, about a mile down the road. It would have to do. I didn't want to get lost in Las Vegas. I had had enough excitement for one day.

I parked my car in the huge Walmart parking lot in a daze. When I came out after shopping, it was getting dark and I couldn't find my car. I looked and looked. No green Jeep. I began to cry. I felt helpless and hopeless. I was tired, sore and dirty. My family was waiting in a hospital. My dog was in Death Valley, and my RV had burned down, almost causing me to lose my son, again! Now I had lost the Jeep.

"Please God, help me. I can't take much more," I prayed.

Then I found it! Right where I had left it, just a short walk from where I had broken down in tears.

Happy to be back in the car, I drove back to the hospital to get Mark and Mario. When I gave Mark the clothes, he said, "Walmart clothes?"

Mark likes to shop Macys. I told him not to be so picky. I was tired, and it was the best I could do. They changed in the hospital restroom, then we went out for Mexican food, Mark's favorite.

After dinner we decided to get a nice room at the Luxor Hotel.

The insurance could pick up the tab. The Luxor is world famous. It is shaped like an Egyptian pyramid with a beam of white light shooting out of the top. I have been told that the astronauts can see the Luxor light from the space station. Since we didn't have a Las Vegas map, the Luxor light was our beacon to a comfortable bed and a good night's sleep.

At about 10:00 p.m. we drove up to the front of the Luxor.

"Oh no, we can't go in there! Look at all the limos!" I exclaimed.

Women in evening gowns and men in suits were parading into the Luxor's front door. We were in Walmart clothes, with dirty shoes, covered in smoke. We looked homeless. Where was the back entrance?

Finally, after driving around some more, we found a parking garage and the back entrance. We loaded up Mario with our Walmart bags and pushed his wheelchair through the casino to the check-in desk. We must have been quite a sight. To our amazement we got a room with two queen size beds and a wheelchair accessible shower for sixty-nine dollars!

After a shower, we tucked Mario into bed. He wanted to know where his Teddy bear was.

"Remember the RV fire Mario? We are in Las Vegas, no Teddy tonight. Now go to sleep, we will go back to Death Valley tomorrow." I said.

It was 12:00 p.m. when Mark and I finally got to bed. What a day! I wondered what tomorrow would bring.

Before falling asleep, Mark and I talked. We were so grateful to be alive. What if the fire had started in the night? Ten seconds longer at the store or a visit to the horses, and it would have been curtains for Mario. What should we do now? Salvage what we could and go home with our tails between our legs? No, we both decided to continue our vacation and keep a good attitude.

The next morning we rented a U-Haul trailer. Hopefully, some of our stuff would be OK. After breakfast at the Luxor we got a phone call. The fire had restarted in the night and it was feared that all of our possessions were lost. Oh well, Mario was still alive, and that's what mattered. Mark and I talked some more and thought the U-Haul was still a good idea. Surely some of the camping equipment in the storage compartments would be all right.

The Jeep needed to be wired for the U-Haul so it would be an hour or so before it was ready. That gave me some time to buy more supplies and a little food. We didn't want to eat out all the time. Buying breakfast and lunch food would be enough. Dinners we could eat out.

To my amazement, one block from the U-Haul store was a Trader Joe's, my favorite store. I went shopping while Mark waited for the Jeep with Mario.

When we got back to Death Valley that night we checked into the Furnace Creek Ranch. Luckily they had a room. It was almost Christmas, the busiest time of year. We soon discovered that Mario was famous. Everyone around Furnace Creek knew about the RV fire and the disabled boy that narrowly escaped death. News travels fast in Death Valley. We were told that the fire incident was even on the Internet.

We had a delicious dinner, and Mario made friends with the waitress, Sam. We tried to eat in Sam's section every night for the rest of the vacation.

A Christmas parade was coming up on Christmas Eve, and Sam offered to help me with Mario so he could be in the parade. I had lights on his wheelchair and antlers for Sola. Mario wore all red and a Santa hat. He took first place in the parade! His trophy sits proudly in his bedroom.

When we went back to campsite #118, we were surprised to find out that all was not lost in the fire. All of the camping equipment was spared, along with our wedding rings, Mario's journal, and our camera. It took us several hours to rummage through all the debris. Now I had some idea of what other fire and flood victims went through, except this was our RV, not our home.

Mario sat in the car and listened to a book-on-tape while we salvaged our stuff. After about an hour of listening to the tape, it stopped.

"Mark something is wrong with the tape player." I yelled. Mark came out to check.

" Shit!" Mark exclaimed. The Jeep battery was dead.

"But we just had it checked in Barstow. How could that be?" I asked.

"Shit happens!" Mark replied.

I went right back to good attitude and gratitude.

"At least it didn't die on the way to Las Vegas, or when we were out four-wheeling on some back country road. We are safe, and there is a gas station just down the road," I reminded him.

Mark got on the bicycle and went to the gas station. I took Mario on a walk and made him lunch.

When Mark got to the gas station he began talking to the attendant, a "good old boy" who looked like he had just crawled out from under an engine. He probably had.

Harry was as thin as a rail, with black car grease on his hands and under his nails. He wore grey coveralls, a lot like the blue suits we used to dress Mario in when he was pulling out feeding tubes. Mark had just finished telling Harry about the RV fire story, saying "Shit happens!" when Harry interrupted him.

"There is a proper way to say that. It's poop! Poop happens. When I was a kid, our house burned down and all that they could save was our 1819 Smith & Wesson rifle and a bible. The Lord protected our most precious processions," Harry said.

There were many more adventures in Death Valley, and Mario continued to make new friends wherever he went. It turned out that the Santa in the annual Christmas parade was the same volunteer firefighter chief that had put out the RV fire and investigated the cause. He took many pictures of Mario in the parade and burned them onto a CD, which he gave us.

I have found people to be helpful and loving wherever we go. When you need help, most people are willing to give it. The universe truly does provide everything you need. All you need to do is ask and be ready to receive.

CHAPTER 29

The Magic Rock

Let me love like I have never been hurt.
Let me sing and dance without a care.
Let me live like my heaven is on Earth.
And so it is.

Quote from the Divine Source

Another place we like to take Mario camping is Lake Siskiyou, by the "City of Mt. Shasta." We discovered it while driving back from our Oregon vacation in July 2002, just before the accident.

Resting at the headwaters of the Sacramento River, this little lake is a jewel. The water is clean and full of life. You can view all kinds of fish if you put on a snorkel and mask and go swimming. Only small fishing boats, kayaks or canoes are allowed. A five MPH speed limit is strictly enforced.

From the shore of the lake you have an awesome view of sacred Mt. Shasta. The campground is privately run and offers two nice handicapped campsites with hookups. We have camped at both sites.

Another helpful feature is the boat launch. A disabled parking spot is right next to the launch and just a few feet from a fishing dock and swimming area.

Besides horseback riding and horse camping, Mark and I enjoy biking and kayaking. At Lake Siskiyou we can do both, so we wanted to see if we could get Mario into a kayak safely. It would be a wonderful experience for him if we could manage it.

Just before the trip to Lake Siskiyou we purchased a yellow tandem thirteen-foot Ocean Kayak. This large two-person kayak was big enough for Mark and our two dogs plus me. When we are not kayaking with Mario we always take Sola and Igo (our new dog). This kayak is so stable that you can stand up in it without tipping. Mario cannot swim, so we had to make sure the kayak was stable and that he was fitted with a good life jacket.

It took a lot of patience and three people to get Mario into the kayak the first time. One person held the boat steady while the other two assisted Mario in walking down to the boat launch. We have found it easiest to wade Mario knee deep into the water and then turn him sideways, sit him down, and lift his legs into the boat. Once in the kayak, Mark grabs him by the armpits and lifts him up into a proper sitting position.

It is hard for Mario to stay in a good sitting position. After about ten minutes he begins to slip down into a recumbent position. It is not ideal, but it works. Mario has a lightweight oar and is able to paddle some. That first day Mario stayed out in the boat for about two hours! He really enjoyed this kayak experience.

Getting Mario out and doing things is one of the reasons he keeps improving. He loves people and thrives on new experiences. Many times disabled people are afraid to go out in public. They often become overly self-conscious. It is beneficial to their healing to get out. They should be encouraged to go out and try new things. I think it is even harder for the people with TBI or adult onset injuries, because they remember how they were before the illness or accident. This is a big challenge and that is when family and friends can help the most with their love, ideas, and encouragement. Amazing things can happen with a little help from family and friends. Mario is proof of that.

One day, when we went down to take Mario for a swim, we noticed that the disabled parking spot was taken. Oh no! What were we going to do? The regular parking lot was up a steep hill. Parking there would mean dropping Mario off, unpacking all the stuff, wheelchair, urinal, fins, snorkels, masks, walker, chairs, food, drinks, dogs, pillows, towels, and blanket, and then moving the car. That was lot of extra work that we didn't want to do. Also, it would be a hassle to get Mario to the restroom without the Jeep. We could use the urinal, but what if he had to have a bowel movement? With Mario you just never know what to expect. The restrooms were at the top of a very steep hill. Funny how hills that I never even noticed before now presented such an obstacle.

I looked around and saw a middle-aged man at a table playing cards with a little old lady. Maybe they were the ones in our spot.

" Excuse me, sir. Is that your car parked in the disabled parking spot?" I inquired.

"Yes it is," replied the man.

"Would you mind if we park behind you until you leave? We have a severely disabled son and we want to take him swimming," I explained.

"Sure, no problem. We will be leaving soon anyway," he responded.

We pulled in behind the man's car and started unpacking. First we let out the dogs, and then we unpacked the gear. Mario would be last. After setting up everything, Mark and I went to get Mario out of the Jeep. He wanted to swim, but first he needed to pee. Not wanting to drive up the hill, we draped towels around Mario and used a urinal. This was one of those times I was grateful to have a son instead of a daughter. Male plumbing is so much easier to deal with, and so discrete.

After taking care of business, Mark and I put Mario's reef walkers on and hand-walked him over river rock and to the water's edge, not an easy task. Once by the water, I put Mario's wet suit vest and life jacket on him. He gets cold easily and the neoprene vest helps keep him warm. A wetsuit or swimming shirt are both very good ideas for the disabled, or anyone with poor circulation.

Mario loved the water and practiced floating on his back while moving his arms and legs. A couple of times Mario stopped because he wanted to dunk his face in the water. We moved him to the dock where he could hold onto the edge, plug his nose, and dunk his head under the water. Mario played in the water for about thirty minutes. Little did we know we were being watched the entire time.

When Mario started to shiver I knew it was time to get him out of the water. I called Mark over and we waddled Mario over the rocks, inch by inch, to a canvas camping chair. Plop! Down he went into the chair, but oh no, he had to pee again! While sitting down covered with towels, Mario relieved himself. Thank God again for portable urinals!

Mario would never consider going pee in a lake. As small children,

I had programmed both my boys to never pee in the water. That meant swimming pools, lakes, rivers, and the ocean.

We had just finished taking care of business when I looked up and saw the nice man coming down the hill.

"Are you leaving now?" I asked. "I will get my keys and move the Jeep."

"Wait!" he said.

The man walked closer, held out his hand and introduced himself. "My name is Ted and I just wanted to thank you."

"Thank me?" I thought.

"I have been watching you and your husband with your son, and I am deeply touched by all the love you have for him. I am a caregiver for that elderly woman you see over there. Her name is Alice.

"I too have experienced a life challenge. After serving in Vietnam I got very sick. The doctors could not figure out what was wrong with me. After many years of suffering I moved to Mt. Shasta City and began studying the healing arts. I slowly got better and am now a caregiver myself," he shared.

"Never give up hope and don't listen to the doctors," he cautioned.

I told him Mario's story, after introducing the family. I shared with Ted how far Mario had come, against all odds. I told him that we never gave up and that was why he kept getting better. Ted said he would pray for Mario and I thanked him. He shook hands with Mario and Mark, and then Mario insisted on a group hug. Mario loves group hugs.

I moved the Jeep for Ted and he thanked me again. This was the first time in my life that I had been thanked after asking someone to do something for me.

Sometimes allowing others to help you is a gift to them. It goes along with the idea of give a healing, get a healing. Or the more you give, the more you receive. It was a beautiful moment.

After that beautiful moment, it didn't take long for Mario to change the mood into one of frustration. He couldn't find his ring. He started pointing at the water and mumbling, "ring, ring."

"Mario, are you sure you had it on while swimming?" I asked.

"I think you took it off before we came," I mentioned. Mario was getting anxious and moving into a stage two tantrum.

"Okay, calm down. Dad and I will put on our snorkels and masks and look for your ring," I consoled.

"Maybe we can find it in the water," I suggested.

Mark and I looked and looked, but no ring. Mario was now moving into a stage three. We had better get him into the Jeep fast. Mark and I hate public displays of anger.

We loaded up the car first and sent Sola over to try and calm Mario down. She helped. He was down to a stage two. Mark and I walked our raging Godzilla Boy over the river rock and toward the Jeep. On the way to the car a rock distracted Mario. He stopped his ranting and motioned for Mark to pick it up. The rock Mark picked up was small and flat and could easily fit into the palm of your hand. It had an impression that looked like someone had pressed his or her thumb into it.

Mark gave the rock to Mario and said, " Mario look! You found a 'happy rock.' If you put your thumb right here it will make you feel good."

Mario placed his thumb on the rock and began to smile. We kept the "happy rock" close to Mario for the rest of the vacation.

"Maybe we should drill a hole in it and hang it around Mario's neck," I laughed.

His ring was found in the ashtray of the Jeep a few minutes after we got back in it to leave. Mario had put it there before getting out of the car to go swim. All that fuss for nothing.

As Forest Gump would say, "Life is like a box of chocolates, you never know what you're gonna get."

The following summer we again returned to Lake Siskiyou for a ten-day vacation. This time we were joined by two close friends: Sam, a retired schoolteacher, and his wife La Rae.

One day Sam asked Mario what traits he thought were important to have in a woman.

"What kind of woman would you like to have as a girlfriend Mario?" Inquired Sam. Mario pointed to Sam's wife, La Rae.

"Oh no buddy, she is taken," said Sam.

We all laughed, while Mario wrote on his Dynovox computer. "She must have a great smile and attitude about life. Hopefully her parents are alive and will be introduced to my parents so they can be friends. We can have good times together and all eat together and just have a smile together." This was written in July 2007. Not bad for the boy that was called a vegetable.

One day while Mario and I were out taking a walk around the campground, a young boy about twelve came flying past us down a steep hill. He was riding a bike and Mario was in his four-wheel walker.

The boy screamed, "Look out! Here I come!"

I yelled, "Slow down!"

The boy did not slow down and I was pissed. What if he had hit Mario?

I told Mario that some parents just do not train their kids properly.

"What a brat that boy was. He could have hurt us," I lectured.

When we got to the top of the hill, an older couple came out to talk to us. Often, out of the blue, people come over to meet Mario. He is always waving, smiling, and saying "Hi," which attracts a lot of attention.

We introduced ourselves and exchanged stories. This couple told us how their son was diagnosed with autism when just a year or two old. The doctors advised them to institutionalize their son because it would be too difficult to raise him. They refused to do so and worked hard to educate him. He was responding to all their efforts and doing amazing things.

"You might have seen him ride by on his new bike. He just turned twelve and learned to ride a two wheel bike," the wife explained.

We had seen their son, but didn't say a thing. I was eating humble pie. That was the boy who had raced by. The one with "no manners because of bad parenting." Now knowing the truth of the situation, I found it pretty amazing that he called out at all, and didn't just speed by unannounced.

Many times as humans we make judgments from a limited background of knowledge. What you think is the truth, may not be. Don't be too quick to judge.

There are a lot of people in the world just like you that have had their share of challenges. Listen to their stories, share your own; love and support each other. Remember, we are all one.

CHAPTER 30

Mario Sweats the Small Stuff

I have a great plan for the future to help my body and
spread my love to everyone.

Because everyone needs love or a simple smile in their
life.

It feels spectacular!

A really good smile makes you shake uncontrollably
with love for yourself and your creator.

I am going to ask you to pray for the word love.

You need to go out in the world and spread your love
like a virus.

I love you,

Mario

Due to the nature of Mario's brain injury, he can at any given moment
change unexpectedly from the loving person he is into a raging maniac.
He can get worked up about what to us seems trivial. The damage
done to certain areas of the brain can impair the ability to control
impulses. We are often unexpectedly challenged to cope with extremely
frustrating and embarrassing situations. Mario is now obsessive and
compulsive. In this chapter I will share some more experiences we have
gone through while "Raising Mario Twice."

Since the accident Mario has had some difficulty with incontinence.
Many days he has to use the urinal every hour. When we go out to
dinner or anyplace not near a restroom, we hook him up to a condom
catheter with a leg bag. No one can tell that he is hooked up as long as
he wears long pants, and we don't have the worry of accidents.

At night we keep a urinal by his bed. He usually wakes up to use it, so his bed is dry most mornings. However, if Mario drinks a lot of water before he goes to bed he will have a wet bed in the morning. Not only does the room smell to high heaven, but I get to wash the sheets, pillowcase, blankets, and pajamas. I have tried bed pads and protective under wear, but he usually just pees around them. It is really unnerving to find a wet bed and blankets yet dry protective underwear.

One time, after three nights of a wet bed, I was pretty sure Mario was sneaking water before bedtime. I talked with Mario about the problem. "Mario, you have wet the bed three days in a row now. You know how you don't like to waste energy." Mario is fanatical about turning out lights to avoid wasting energy. "Having to wash your sheets and blankets for three days is a big waste. Not only do you waste water, but soap and electricity too! Do you understand?" Mario nods his head yes. "If you don't drink anything after 9:00 p.m., you should be okay." Mario agrees and gives me a thumb's up. "Tonight no water after 9:00 p.m., okay?"

After dinner I again remind Mario about the water. It is a hot day, so I encourage him to drink a lot before 9:00 p.m. We watched a movie and it was 10:00 p.m., so we started getting Mario ready for bed. On the way to bed Mario signs that he wants a drink of water. "No water, Mario, remember. We talked about it this morning. Nothing to drink after 9:00 p.m. I do not want another wet bed!"

Using his cane, Mario starts heading toward the water container, obviously growing agitated. He points to his tongue. "Mario, you are not going to have a drink. It is too late," I plead. Mario's body starts to shake and beads of sweat are forming on his brow. He grabs a water glass and heads for the sink. I take the glass away. This really shakes him up. He starts yelling and turns around, hobbling toward the icemaker in the refrigerator. I am afraid he might fall, so I call for Mark to get his wheel chair. I block Mario from getting any ice. "Mario, stop it! You are not going to drink."

He is so angry now that he throws himself down to the floor and crawls towards the dogs' water bowl. He yips like a puppy as he moves toward the bowl. I pick up the bowl and again tell Mario, "No More Water Tonight!" Somehow Mark and I lift Mario into the wheel chair, with him kicking and screaming. We wheel him into his room. Once in his room I set Mario onto his bed and tell him to go to sleep. He throws a pillow at me. Mark sees this and screams, "Mario, you do not throw things at your mother!" We both leave the room.

Almost immediately we hear lots of banging and commotion, then WHAM comes a crash at the door. I tread carefully into his room. His small trash-can is lying near the door. Mario is back in his wheelchair moving toward the door. I wheel Mario back to his bed and say: "Mario, we have had it! Do you want to live somewhere else? We are tired of this and if you keep it up we will call the police. What do you think they will do? Now stay in your room and quit throwing things!"

Again I leave the room and Mark and I wait to see what will happen. After about ten minutes of silence we walk back in to check on Mario. He is sweaty but calm. He motions to me for a towel and I get him a wet washcloth to wipe his face. He tells me he needs my love. Reluctantly I give him a hug. He points to his tongue.

"Okay Mario, I will give you one ice cube. You can have as much water as you want in the morning."

Mario motions for Mark to come over and he insists on giving him a shoulder and back massage. Mark too just wants to leave, but lets Mario make amends by giving a massage. After all, Mario is brain injured and he has trouble with anger management. We love him in spite of it.

Train Ride from Hell

While on vacation at Lake Siskiyou, Mark and I decided it would be fun to take Mario on a train ride. There is a three-hour train ride from Yreka with breathtaking views of Mt. Shasta. Yreka is about a thirty-minute drive from our campground. On the way to the train station Mario motioned that he needed to use the urinal, so we pulled off to the side of the road. We were trying to go without a condom catheter and leg-bag.

"Mario, are you sure you have to go?" I asked. He did and filled the urinal with 200 cc of urine. I walked away with the urinal and dumped the contents without thinking. Mario had a look or horror on his face.

"I am sorry Mario. I forgot to let you see it. There were 200 cc. We have a train to catch, so please get in the car so we can go."

Mario got into the car, but suddenly became angry. He began to scream and bang the doors and windows with his first.

"Mario, if you do not stop this we will have to miss the train ride. Now calm down," I pleaded.

After a few minutes Mario dropped to a level two irritation, which was acceptable to us. He is OCD, so what do you expect? I thought.

We arrive at the train station and have about twenty minutes before we need to board. Mark bought the tickets and I wandered around the train station museum with Mario. Mario was happy now, visiting with all the people that were around. Then Mario says he needs to use the restroom.

"Mario you just went, are you sure?" He shows us two fingers, which means he has to go poop. Oh no, this could take a while and the train is going to board in fifteen minutes. "Mark, you take Mario to the bathroom and I will tell the conductor to wait for us. Ten minutes pass and the conductor says, "All aboard."

I am getting anxious about Mario and Mark, and then my cell phone rings. It is Mark. I can hear Mario screaming in the background. "Mario is having a fit. He had diarrhea and got poop everywhere. I am using wet paper towels to clean up. I had to flush the toilet before he was ready. I don't think we can make the train," Mark explained.

"We are going to get on that train! We bought our tickets, now get him out here. I will ask the conductor to wait," I demanded. Poor Mark brought the irate Mario through the train station in his walker, red, sweaty and fuming.

I told the conductor about our situation and how Mario was brain injured and easy to upset. He said, "No problem, the train will wait." When Mario got up to the train door the conductor met him with a handshake.

"Hello Mario, we are happy to have you on our train. Let me help you." After Mario got in, he said, "Listen everyone, this is Mario Scharmer, and he is going to ride with us. Give him a big hand."

Everyone clapped for Mario and he began to wave and smile to all the passengers as he walked down the isle holding onto the seats for balance. We went to the back of the train, as far back as we could go. There were about six open rows of seats. We sat Mario down and thought the whole episode was behind us. It wasn't.

Mario started to think about the flushed poop and began to get angry all over again. The train started moving and we were stuck. "Mario, it's okay. Look, we are moving, this is going to be great!" I announced. Now Mario is kicking at me and starting to make noise.

"Shit! What are we going to do now?" Mark asked.

I continue to try and distract Mario with scenery, to no avail, when two children walk by. They look at Mario and stop for a second. Mario stops too.

"Hi kids, this is Mario, what are your names?" They introduce themselves and give Mario a paper million-dollar bill. Mario kisses their hands and again is beaming from ear to ear. The children leave and Mario starts to get angry all over again. He takes the pencil I gave him to write about his troubles and tries to stab me with it. That's it.

"You are not going to hurt me, Mario. We are leaving. This is the last train trip we are ever going to take you on! Mark let's move. Let the brat ride by himself. I have had it!"

Mark and I move several seats away and hope that the rest of the people on the train are not too disturbed by all the commotion. I try not to look at Mario's contorted facial features. At least he is quiet now. Mark and I ride along for the next thirty minutes, not having any fun, wondering what we should do when the train stops. Hopefully Mario will be over his fit, but who knows.

The train stops at a little town for one hour. Everyone gets off the train, but should we? Mario seems OK and he is probably hungry. I decide to check with him.

"Mario, do you want to get off the train for lunch?" He shakes his head yes. "Okay, but you need to be good. We only have one hour so you will have to get a 'to go' box if you are not finished," I reminded him. Mario never finishes eating in one hour and we don't want to miss our train.

We get off the train and the conductor is so helpful. He says not to worry about a thing. He has a disabled son and knows how hard it can be at times. I thank the man and off we go to lunch. Mario was great at the restaurant and makes friends with the waitress. She tells us how sweet Mario is and how lucky we are to have him. Mark and I look at each other and think: If she only knew.

Fingernails

Mario does not like us to cut his fingernails. When they get too long we usually let him try to trim them himself. With his poor fine motor skills, he sometimes nicks his fingers, plus it takes him a long time. We don't like to let his nails get too long, because they become a hazard when he goes into one of his rages. All of us have been scratched at least once.

It was a Wednesday afternoon, and Mario had an appointment at the rehabilitation facility. He is an out- patient and returns for new therapy about every six months. Because it was a cool day I decided to bring my little dog Igo along. I named her Igo because I take her with me where ever I go. She is a small Schnauzer/Pincher mixed breed. We got her after our return home from Death Valley 2005, the year of the RV fire. I love to joke around with her name ,saying, "Igo, you stay," or "you stay, Igo." She follows me all around the house and we are rarely apart for more than a few hours.

To help save time, I decided to cut Mario's nails on the way to rehab. Eric, Mario's care provider and buddy, drove. We got on the freeway and I explained to Mario what I was about to do. "Mario, your fingernails are really long and need to be cut. I am going to cut them for you, okay?" Mario never really gave permission, but I started cutting anyway. I got the first hand done without much trouble. He did not look happy, so I figured I had better speed things up. I held his other hand and clipped away. Mario started to squirm and fuss. "I am almost done, just a couple of more fingers to do, Mario." Snip, snip, I am now finished.

Mario begins to sweat, squirm, and fuss. He starts to moan. "What's the matter, Mario? Are you upset that I cut your nails?" He starts pounding on the car window with his fist, screaming. Igo tries to escape to the front seat of the car, so I grab her, afraid she will interfere with Eric's driving. Mario starts kicking and hitting the car door. It is only a couple of miles to rehab and there really isn't any place to pull over. I pray he will not open the car door and fall out. I continue to try and calm Mario down. "Mario, I am sorry, I will never cut your fingernails again. Next time you can do it yourself at home," I consoled. I tried singing to Mario. That didn't' work either. If we could make it to rehab, maybe a doctor could shoot him with a dart or something.

We pulled into the parking lot with a screaming Mario, frightened dog, and frazzled mother. "Eric, get his walker. Maybe he will calm down if he moves." Eric pulls the walker out of the trunk and takes it to Mario. I open the door. Sweating and screaming, Mario hangs onto the walker and starts to walk across the parking lot. By the time he gets across he has calmed down. I open the windows and lock the car. Igo will have to stay until the appointment is over.

There were no more problems with Mario for the rest of the day. Sometimes I feel like placing a sign on Mario, "Free to Good Home," and leaving him on a busy street corner somewhere. He was cheerful and pleasant to everyone at rehab, kissing hands, smiling, and cheerful. I wrote down the entire incident in a journal to share with Mario's psychologist at his next therapy session.

At his therapy session his therapist talked with Mario about this outburst and came up with a plan. The plan is for Mario to save his fingernails and feed them to a plant. He doesn't want his fingernails thrown away or wasted. If we save them and give them to a plant, he will not get upset. Now we have a designated plant in our house just for fingernails. I have not had a problem cutting them since we started feeding the plant Mario's nails.

CHAPTER 31

In Reflection

When a life-changing event happens, you feel like life stops, but everything around you continues. People go to work, bills need to be paid, animals fed, houses cleaned, hair washed, teeth brushed, laundry done, etc. It is like having a new baby without the joy of new life. Living in hospital waiting rooms you lose all sense of time. Days and nights are the same. You are living hour to hour, waiting, hoping, and praying for news that will restore your life.

Most people love order and routine. Even if your job, marriage, or home life is unhappy, there is comfort in the routine. Many times people stay in unhappy life situations just for the comfort of knowing the routine. By doing this they think they have some control over what is happening in their lives.

This is an illusion. Life happens. It is always changing. You cannot control life. You can try, by doing all the "safe, right things," but life will just happen. This is why the health nut gets cancer even though he/she ate right and exercised every day. Or the straight-arrow college graduate student with such a promising future gets shot on the way home from work. People die, are born, and get sick or injured. It is just life.

We may ask why. And my answer is, it is just because life happens. I am not saying that our choices don't make a difference. I am saying that you cannot always predict the results your choices will make or what challenges may come your way. What you do have control over is your attitude. How you are going to respond with what does happen in your life each day.

Every morning when you wake up, you get to choose how you are going to greet the day. The magic is your attitude. Attitude not only changes how you feel, but how the people around you react.

When I have a friendly, happy attitude and am ready to receive all the love that the universe has to offer, I meet the most wonderful people, even when I am in a difficult situation. When I am tired, angry, and have a nasty attitude, guess what? I receive angry and nasty right back. Change your attitude and just see how fast your universe can change.

Our friend Richard Carlson said to his wife Kris, just a few months before his death, "Kris you know what I love most about the human spirit? People experience tragedy, and it makes their life have greater meaning."

Life is not always easy, but if you go with the flow and focus on the good stuff, you can have a magical, wonderful, fulfilling life. Now all I want to do is be healthy, have fun new experiences, and spread the love that I have for people, life, animals, and the planet.

Every day we continue to have amazing adventures with Mario. Although at times life with Mario is very challenging, it is so often magical. While I would not wish misfortune on anyone, sometimes our greatest growth comes out of a tragedy.

Recently Miguel asked me, "Mom, if you could go back in time and change events in your life, would you?"

I have seriously thought about this question and certainly would love to prevent any injury from happening to either of my children. But if I changed past events, where would we be today? Life might be easier, but it could also be harder. No, I think the past is best left alone. I prefer to work in the ever present now.

The experience of raising Mario twice has been a life enriching one, not only for me, but also for the hundreds of people who have been around Mario. How our lives would have changed if Mario or his brother had listened to the woman who told them not to go out that night.

What if the accident had happened before everyone in the truck had been dropped off? How many of Mario's friends might have been killed or injured?

As bad as things were for my family and me, we still have a lot to be grateful for. So many worse things could have happened that night with these two wild partying boys. Something bad was bound to happen to someone sooner or later.

I have no regrets now and look forward to each day and all the possibilities for the future. Mario has taught me to live in the now and I am a happier person because of it.

It turns out that Mario is my greatest teacher. I have become a wiser woman. One never knows where their wisdom may arise. I certainly didn't plan on any of this happening.

Currently Mario is receiving acupuncture, speech therapy, chiropractic and mental health services from our HMO. He is being fitted for a splint to help work on straightening his right arm. He is having toe surgery to release a locked joint. None of these services were suggested to us; we had to ask for them all.

Mario got glasses. We had to ask. He got his hearing checked. We had to ask. He got a standing frame. We had to ask. He got a four-wheel walker. We had to ask for it. His Dynovox communication device at the expense of $10,000. We had to ask, push, and demand to get it. We received one after two years. The list goes on, but I think you get the picture. Ask and you shall receive. Don't give up.

Now, in 2009, we are working on independence. I am filling out applications and researching housing so Mario can live on his own in the next few years. There are waiting lists for these places, so you have to get started early. It is a lot of work, but it has to be done.

We can finally see, after seven years of hard work, the possibility of Mario living on his own, with assistance. In Home Support Services (IHSS) workers are available to help him with cooking, laundry, and taking him to appointments. To make it easier for Mario to be independent, we are going to ask our HMO to provide Mario with an electric scooter or electric wheelchair, so he can get around easier. We will continue to work on his walking, but his balance is so poor at this time, it would not be safe for him to be in an apartment alone in a walker. Maybe we can find a roommate to live with Mario.

At one of his psychotherapy sessions Mario wrote what he thinks he needs to be able to do before living on his own.

He wrote: "I want to cook. I'd like my brother to teach me. Manage my anger, learn to work on the computer (I'm taking little steps.), I need to do laundry (maybe my brother can teach me). I will need help with: Going places and driving. I forgot how to drive. I need someone to shop for food. Help with cleaning, and someone to walk with me."

Before this time we couldn't even imagine independence, but now after seven years we have some goals and objectives. In the beginning we couldn't think of the future and had to stay in the moment to survive. After many years and much healing we have found a balance between living in the now and planning for the future.

When meeting with Mario's social worker, he pointed out how important it is to try to get any disabled family member independent if you can. The odds are that the parents will die before their disabled child. What would happen to Mario if we both died? We want Mario to have a happy life and live in a comfortable situation. It is important that we do make some plans for his future. A will alone is not enough.

It is a little scary thinking about moving Mario out on his own, because we love him so much. We have been through a lot together. It was our love and hard work that brought him this far. We will always be in Mario's life as long as we are alive, but what a wonderful thing for Mario, to have his own place! How and when we make the transition to independence is yet to be determined. Remember to set your goals and never give up hope. Hope is often what keeps us all going.

One sleepless night I got up to meditate and began to feel overwhelmed with love. During the experience I realized how all I have ever wanted in my life was love. The funny thing is, I have been surrounded with love my entire life. I started to feel the love of all the people in my lifetime. First I felt the love of Sai Baba in India, a holy man that I had visited in 1979. That was my first experience of timeless, unconditional love. I basked in the warm flow of love that Baba had for me. I cried tears of bliss in a timeless state of ecstasy.

Next I felt the love of my mother, father, brother, and two sons, Mario and Miguel. The love kept flowing like a river, faster and faster, endlessly flowing.

I started remembering how many people had loved me, friends at school, students, and teachers. I remembered Mario's accident and the love I had received from Virginia, Nancy, Mario's girls, Richard and Kris Carlson, my brother, family members, and even the medical staff, like Solon, Dr. K., Dr. A., and Dr. F.

Then I thought of Mark Scharmer, my rock. Mark my husband. The man who always has a hug for me. The man who stands by me, always comforting me, no matter how bitchy or emotional I am. He is there, no matter how late at night it is or how tired he might be. Mark, so even, so patient, and so loving. How grateful I am for Mark.

And of course the animals, I cannot forget the animals. Mochi and Freesia, who no matter how tired we were, or what time of night we returned home, greeted us with wagging tails and soft wet tongues.

Sola, who as a puppy not only tolerated the rough touch of a disabled young man, but also returned so much unconditional love to all of us and still does.

Igo, my little lap dog who follows me everywhere and looks up to me like a Goddess and sees the love that I am.

The horses that empowered me and took us away from all the stresses of life on our wild and free rides through the woods. So much love, I am bursting with love.

Tears are now streaming down my face as I reflect and feel all the love. That's it. That is the secret to happiness. To be love. That is how I want to live the rest of my life, surrounded by love.

Why limit yourself to being in love with one person when you can be love with the world. Expand the feeling of love for yourself and all of life and you will have the bliss that you deserve. We are all one and in that oneness we can experience the ultimate bliss. To be love or not to be love, that is the question.

Life is so easy! Life is so good!

All good things come to me!

This is a magnificent Universe.

The Universe is bringing all good things to me.

The Universe is conspiring for me at all times!

The Universe is supporting me in everything I do!

The Universe meets all my needs immediately!

Be Love

By Doc and Leslie